The Afghanistan Poppy
Eradication Campaign

ALSO BY OR EDITED BY HARRY SPILLER
AND FROM MCFARLAND

*Veterans of Iraq and Afghanistan:
Personal Accounts of 22 Americans Who Served* (2014)

*Support Programs for Ex-Offenders:
A State-by-State Directory* (2011)

*American POWs in World War II: Twelve Personal Accounts
of Captivity by Germany and Japan* (2009)

*Pearl Harbor Survivors:
An Oral History of 24 Servicemen* (2002)

*Prisoners of Nazis: Accounts by American POWs
in World War II* (edited, 1998)

*American POWs in Korea:
Sixteen Personal Accounts* (edited, 1998)

*Scars of Vietnam: Personal Accounts
by Veterans and Their Families* (1994, softcover 2012)

*Death Angel: A Vietnam Memoir of a Bearer
of Death Messages to Families* (1992, softcover 2012)

The Afghanistan Poppy Eradication Campaign

*Accounts from the Black Hawk
Counter-Narcotics Infantry
Kandak Team in Helmand Province*

HARRY SPILLER

McFarland & Company, Inc., Publishers
Jefferson, North Carolina

Library of Congress Cataloguing-in-Publication Data

Names: Spiller, Harry, 1945– author.
Title: The Afghanistan poppy eradication campaign : accounts from the Black Hawk Counter-Narcotics Infantry Kandak Team in Helmand Province / Harry Spiller.
Description: Jefferson, North Carolina : McFarland & Company, Inc., Publishers, 2017 | Includes bibliographical references and index.
Identifiers: LCCN 2017033035 | ISBN 9781476668642 (softcover : acid free paper) ♾
Subjects: LCSH: Afghan War, 2001—-Campaigns—Afghanistan—Helmand. | Opium trade—Afghanistan. | Drug traffic—Afghanistan. | Opium poppy—Control—Afghanistan—Helmand. | Military assistance, American—Afghanistan—Helmand. | Helmand (Afghanistan)—History, Military.
Classification: LCC DS371.412 .S695 2017 | DDC 958.104/71—dc23
LC record available at https://lccn.loc.gov/2017033035

British Library cataloguing data are available

ISBN (print) 978-1-4766-6864-2
ISBN (ebook) 978-1-4766-2810-3

© 2017 Harry Spiller. All rights reserved

No part of this book may be reproduced or transmitted in any form or by any means, electronic or mechanical, including photocopying or recording, or by any information storage and retrieval system, without permission in writing from the publisher.

Front cover photographs: Poppy field near Nad Ali; Pogue Mahone cougar hits IED (photographs by Greg Strong); background © 2017 iStock

Printed in the United States of America

McFarland & Company, Inc., Publishers
 Box 611, Jefferson, North Carolina 28640
  www.mcfarlandpub.com

To all the men and women
of the Armed Forces and their families
who have served in Afghanistan

Acknowledgments

I would like to thank Major Greg Settle for providing the army records of Counter Narcotics Infantry Kandak Embedded Training Team (CNIK ETT) in Afghanistan during 2008 and 2009. I would also like to thank Kurt Merseal, Greg Settle, Jason Williams, Troy Kemper, Adam Cole, Kyle Campbell, Jeffery Sowash, James Ressel, John Sury, Brian Mays, and Greg Strong for sharing their experiences from their poppy eradication mission in Helmand Province. In addition, I thank Jenifer Pritchard from the Williamson County Sheriff's Department for her research. Without their help, this book would not have been possible.

Table of Contents

Acknowledgments	vi
Introduction	1
One. The Arrival	5
Two. The Ambush	21
Three. Afghanistan National Army 2 KIAs	32
Four. It Was 75 Meters Away	46
Five. Within Inches	56
Six. AT4 Round Misses Compound	70
Seven. The IEDs	80
Eight. Smoke Signals	91
Nine. The Black Hawks Find the Largest IED Factory in Afghanistan	97
Ten. The Last Days	120
Eleven. Five Years Later	128
Appendix	151
Chapter Notes	157
References	159
Index	161

Introduction

Afghanistan is a mountainous, landlocked country located between Pakistan to the east and Iran to the west, with a population of roughly 30 million of the poorest, least educated, most battle-scarred people on Earth. It has been called the "Graveyard of Empires" because so many invading armies and would-be occupiers have foundered within its borders. In the 1980s the United States, Saudi Arabia, and Pakistan supported an insurgency in Afghanistan against a Soviet puppet government. As the Afghan government began to lose control of the provinces during the Soviet invasion of 1979–1980, warlords flourished, along with opium production as regional commanders searched for ways to generate money to purchase weapons. At this time the United States pursued an arms-length strategy of supporting the Afghan freedom fighters (or Mujahideen), the main purpose being to cripple the Soviet Union slowly into withdrawal through attrition rather than effecting a quick and decisive overthrow. The Soviets alleged on several occasions that American CIA agents were helping to smuggle opium out of Afghanistan, either into the West (in order to raise money for Afghan resistance) or into the Soviet Union (in order to weaken it through drug addiction). In 1989 the Soviets withdrew, and with that victory American interest in the country waned for a time.

When the Soviet Union was forced to withdraw from Afghanistan in 1989, a power vacuum was created. Various Mujahideen factions started fighting each other for power. With the discontinuation of Western support, they resorted more frequently to poppy cultivation to finance their military endeavors. Ultimately, one faction, the Taliban, seized control of Afghanistan.

Introduction

In July 2000, Taliban leader Mullah Mohammed Omar, collaborating with the United Nations in an effort to eradicate heroin production in Afghanistan, declared that growing poppies was un-Islamic, resulting in one of the world's most successful anti-drug campaigns. The Taliban enforced a ban on poppy farming via threats, forced eradication, and public punishment of transgressors. The result was a 99 percent reduction of opium poppy farming in Taliban-controlled areas—roughly three-quarters of the world's supply of heroin at the time. However, the ban was effective only for a short time due to the subsequent deposition of the Taliban following the terrorist attacks of 9/11 and the U.S. invasion of Afghanistan.

Some individuals believe that certain parties benefited from the price increase of heroin during the ban, even going so far as to argue that it was a form of market manipulation on the part of certain drug lords. Dried opium, unlike most agricultural products, can easily be stored for long periods without refrigeration or other expensive equipment. With huge stashes of opium stored in secret hideaways, the Taliban and other groups that became involved in the drug trade were able to reap huge personal profits during the price spikes after the 2000 ban and the chaos of 9/11.

Afghanistan has been the greatest illicit opium producer in the entire world, ahead of the "Golden Triangle" (i.e., the shared border area between Myanmar, Laos, and Thailand) and Latin America since 1992. Opium production has been on the rise since U.S. occupation of Afghanistan started in 2001. Based on United Nations Office on Drugs and Crime (UNODC) data, there has been significant opium poppy cultivation in each of four growing seasons during 2004–2007.

In 2007, 92 percent of the *non-pharmaceutical-grade* opiates on the world market originated in Afghanistan. This amounts to an export value of $4 billion, a quarter of which is earned by opium farmers, with the rest going to district officials, insurgents, warlords, and drug traffickers. In the seven years prior to the Taliban opium ban in 2000, the Afghan farmers' share of gross income from opium was divided among 200,000 families. In addition to opiates, Afghanistan is the largest producer of cannabis in the world.

The United States, in conjunction with the Afghanistan National

Introduction

Army's Counter Narcotics Infantry Kandak (ANA CNIK), began to conduct joint operations of poppy eradication in the country. In April 2009, the Illinois Army National Guard, 2nd Battalion, 130th Infantry Regiment, 33rd Infantry Brigade Combat Team (consisting of sixteen soldiers), was mobilized and deployed to Afghanistan as the Counter Narcotics Infantry Kandak Embedded Training Team (CNIK ETT). The sixteen-man team, along with ANA CNIK, the Afghanistan National Police's Poppy Eradication Force and DynCorp International's Poppy Eradication Force, was assigned to Helmand Province with plans to eradicate poppy cultivation and support the national goals for reducing illicit crop production.

The CNIK ETT was involved in more than one hundred combat operations over the course of the team's deployment. During the seventy-five days in which they operated in Helmand, forty operations were directly related to the eradication mission. Thirty-one of those operations involved direct engagements with enemy forces for more than fifty continuous hours of fighting. Typical engagements by the enemy were with AK-47s, RPGs, PKMs and 82mm mortars. Several assaults included 107mm rockets and a ZSU-23 anti-aircraft gun. In addition to the many rocket attacks on the force while conducting the eradication missions, 10 rockets and an unknown number of mortars were fired on Forward Observation Base (FOB) Eagle. The team successfully detected 4 improvised explosive devices (IEDs) that were neutralized by the DynCorp Explosive Ordnance Disposal (EOD) team. They also experienced one IED strike with no casualties or injuries.

Official reports state that thirty-nine Taliban fighters were killed and fourteen detainees were taken by the CNIK. However, based on reports from various sources (radio and television, chatter from local Taliban fighters, and Afghanistan National Security Forces), the actual number of enemy fighters killed was closer to 150, with two of them (Khadahari and Mullah Abdullah) being local Taliban commanders. Of the fourteen detainees, one was suspected of being high-ranking fighter, as his cell phone had recordings of him delivering various speeches.

The CNIK team was highly successful during its operations in Helmand, locating (and later burning) approximately 11.2 tons of poppy

Introduction

seed and discovering an IED factory. The factory had an immense store of bomb-making materials and explosives that were linked to the IED strikes against one or more of the team's vehicles. It was suspected that the factory, in addition to being linked to a large number of IED strikes in the area, was the largest single IED factory in Afghanistan.

I felt this story was unique and needed to be told. The men of the Counter Narcotics Infantry Kandak Embedding Training Team began a difficult task after learning that the team they were relieving had lost half of its men. On top of dealing with rain, mud, cold weather, hot weather of more than 100 degrees, and horrible living conditions coupled with cultural differences, this class-A army unit, well trained and disciplined with a "we've got to get this done" attitude, was tasked with training the Afghanistan National Army, poorly trained with a "we no do that today" attitude. In addition, there was the concern of ANA soldiers who had family members who were part of the Taliban (or were possibly Taliban themselves). Yet the team completed its mission.

During the 75-day eradication operation, the Afghanistan National Army had eight soldiers wounded in action. In addition, Shams Ullaq, Aman Ullah, and PSG Lal Mohammad of the Afghan forces were killed in action. Though engaged in daily fire fights for 75 days, expending 12,000 .50 caliber rounds; 1,857 MK-19 grenades; 8,150 heavy and light machine-gun rounds; 1,200 M-4 carbine rifle rounds; 200 40mm grenades; and 300 82mm mortars, the Illinois National Guard Counter Narcotics Infantry Kandak Combat Team sustained no casualties. As one team member said, "Sixteen went and sixteen returned!" This is their story.

ONE

The Arrival

"Well today God was keeping me safe. I was driving the Cougar from FOB Dylan to Lashkar Gah. There were times that I was sure I was going to slide right into a canal. On the bright and cheering side I did get to pull down a concrete pole and pull a cougar out of a ditch. [...] We are staying the night at Lashkar Gah and the food is excellent. Tomorrow we escort back thirty more tractors to use to eradicate poppy. One cool thing is that when I see a shepherd herding sheep or look at the mud complexes/ houses, I think how biblical these people are. I mean it is like I am in biblical times."— Lieutenant Troy Kemper

November 2008—Kabul, Afghanistan

The Black Hawk Counter Narcotics Infantry Kandak (CNIK) arrived in Kabul in November 2008. It was cold and rainy. One of the first things that the men noticed was the smell, which had a slight overtone of sewage. The team members were transported to Camp Phoenix, where they settled in for a few days, and then the eradication team moved to a small camp outside of Kabul Camp Dubs. The Afghanistan National Army unit had a small camp next to the Black Hawk team.

Major Kurt Merseal was assigned the mission of assembling a sixteen-man team (the CNIK), which would aid the Afghanistan National Police's Poppy Eradication Force (ANP PEF) and DynCorp International's Poppy Eradication Force in eliminating poppy cultivation and supporting the national goals of reducing illicit crop production. Ideally, one American truck would be assigned to each Afghan company, and security would be set up in a rectangle two kilometers

The Afghanistan Poppy Eradication Campaign

by two kilometers; the Americans would have three sides of the area, and DynCorp would have the fourth. Once the security lines were set up, DynCorp would go inside and eradicate the poppy plants. The Black Hawks were also to mentor the Afghanistan National Army during the operations. However, before eradication could begin, Major Merseal had to train the soldiers of the Afghan army and develop a working relationship with his men and the Afghan soldiers.

Major Kurt Merseal

"The first thing I did was try to find the lieutenant colonel that had the mentoring team in place when we got there. The colonel had been with the Afghans for almost a year on the eradication mission. We found him in a little camp on the outskirts of Kabul. I wanted to get the transition started as soon as possible. The first encounter with them was just gut-wrenching—it was an eye opener. When you first looked at the colonel, he looked like a fast tracker, top of his game, squared-away soldier, but then after a brief encounter we realized he was a spent man. He was done. He had a rough year in country, and half of his team was killed in action. He was done. He had a rough year in country and had had no idea what he was getting into when he was assigned the mission. We talked with him and tried to get information to better prepare our team. We found out that the structure of the Afghan army was different than ours in that the Afghan army answered directly to the minister of defense. The minister of defense is like the American secretary of defense, so they were lightly political. They had a light battalion unit called the Kandak, and there was only one of them in the whole Afghan army. They were the elite of the elite, a unit of Counter Narcotics Infantry Kandak task's with the core mission to support the poppy eradication force to go into rural areas and provide security for the police to go in one field after the other and mow the poppy plants down. The problem in Afghanistan going into that country and taking the poppy is like going to Iowa and taking their corn. The Afghanistan government appeared to support the eradication because of American influences, but it was in a passive way. The Afghan unit had all the good soldiers desert. They had a shell of a unit, and basically they didn't have the equipment, they didn't have the training;

most of them didn't care or want to be there. We found out that it wasn't the farmers who wanted to grow the poppy. They were forced to by the Taliban. We were going to have the same problem the Russians had when they were there. They wanted the farmers to grow wheat. The farmers take the wheat and then the Taliban come in and take the wheat and make them grow poppy. Then the Taliban use the wheat and the fertilizer to make bombs to use against us. After listening to him and seeing how spent he was, his demeanor, and his account, it was quite a sobering moment. It was like, man, we had no idea what we have gotten into."

One thing was for sure: Major Merseal had to go back and tell his team about the shit sandwich they had just received.

First Lieutenant Adam Cole

"The major got the team together and give us this big speech. He started it off with 'Well, boys, we just got handed a shit sandwich and we're going to eat it, and all we can do is make it taste good. The other unit, from the Oregon National Guard, lost 50 percent of their men, so look to your left and then look to your right; one of those guys is gonna be fucking gone.' It scared the hell out of me, and no one left in the Oregon unit could help us as far as a hand off. We just had to deal with it. I had the laziest company commander. He would literally fall asleep in class. The Afghan battalion commander would yell at him and scream at him in the meeting because he just kept falling asleep. I mean, he was just worthless."

Sergeant First Class Greg Strong

"We went into the tent and met the commander from the team that we were relieving. We asked him, 'What are the rules of engagement (ROE) in the south?' He said, 'By God, it's whatever you can live with,' and we're like looking at each other like 'what the fuck's he saying?' When we left Major Merseal said, 'That is bullshit. I am telling you right now we aren't what you can get by with; we will follow the ROE to the letter. That was, if they are shooting at you tear them apart, let them have it, but don't be murdering anybody.'"

The Afghanistan Poppy Eradication Campaign

The Training

Major Kurt Merseal

"We started our training first by attending a counterinsurgency academy, and at that point we met our Afghanistan Kandak. What we found was pretty much everyone on the team had checked out. They were done. They were spent and had done what they needed to do, but they weren't much help to us. The majority of the good ones had deserted; it was a shell of a unit. They didn't have the equipment, they didn't have the training; most of them didn't care and didn't want to be there. They didn't even have a commander, but they had an intern commander that was truly just a political appointment, and he didn't give a shit, so it took us weeks to get a commander, executive officer and company commanders to start building a battalion. We took the approach that we were mentors. It would have been a lot easier if we had just made their commanders puppets and gone in and done all of the missions ourselves. We refused to do that in the spirit of being an advisor and trying to develop the institutional knowledge. We spent a lot of frustrating hours and days. I mentored the battalion commander, who had been in the Afghan army forever. He had had a Russian mentor back in the days when the Russians were there, and he had seen more mentors than you could imagine. I had my executive officer mentor their executive officer. As a result, we developed a trust, and that trust kept them on our side. I think the relationship prevented them from letting things happen to us. We bonded because I didn't tell him what to do. I would make recommendations; I would set the conditions and try to guide him down the path instead of telling him how to do things."

A common term used was "left seat, right seat." This referred to one soldier training another for a particular task. Major Merseal was in the right seat when it came to learning to drive the MRAP Cougar.

"On the first day of training we were going to driver's training. We had these big trucks we had received, and this guy was going to show me how to drive it. I was driving behind the camp, and I didn't know it, but there were mine fields everywhere that the Russians had left when they pulled out. All the locals—the kids, sheep herders, everybody—knew where they walk and where they couldn't walk. We were climbing up this mountain in the truck, and you get on top of the mountain and there is a big flat spot called a range. We were going to drive up to the range. We were on our way, and we saw a bunch of French soldiers in the area. They went flying by us in trucks, and I wondered why they were in such a big hurry. As we were going up the road, they had blocked it with their trucks. I pulled up behind them, and the guy tells me to just go around them. I started to drive around them, and I look over to the side, and I see one of the French. He was all busted up. I knew something wasn't right, and I look over about another 30 yards and see another French soldier that is missing from the waist down. They were new to the area and started walking through this mine field and had cooked off some mines. This guy is telling me to just go around the other trucks, and I said, 'Hey, we are driving through a mine field.' That's how I got introduced with these guys; it was a real eye opener.

"The training was frustrating: you have a team of soldiers that are on top of their game, and you're trying to literally train a group of kindergarteners at times. I mean, it was just chaos. Everything we did was chaotic, and trying to bring organization to those guys and knowing where we were getting ready to go, one of the roughest places in Afghanistan Helmand Province, and knowing what our mission was, and to try to make an elite team out of such a broken unit seemed impossible at times."

Sergeant First Class Greg Strong

"The problem with Afghan soldiers is that they aren't very good shots. Part of the problem is that the AK-47s they had have fold-out stocks instead of wooden stocks on their rifles. It makes it difficult to be a good shot. The Afghanistan National Army (ANA) listen well, but the problem is that they are 80 percent illiterate. On the other hand, they can read you other problems as well. They aren't very clean people, although they do wash their feet before they pray. Their weapons were often dirty and jammed. Another problem was they had no organizational skills. We are very organized, and they don't understand it."

The Afghanistan Poppy Eradication Campaign

First Lieutenant Adam Cole

"We started our training doing classes, PT, firearms training, and map reading, just trying to get ready for the trip down south for poppy season. It was during that time that we had some really stupid things happen. We were trying to get a Raven (a remote-controlled plane with a camera) so we could use it for surveillance. They sent us two PFCs [privates first class] who were Raven operators, but with no Raven.

"That's how we picked up Tyminsky. He was a brand new kid on the block and kind of chubby kid, but seemed like he was going to be all right. Garcia didn't have an MOS, but he had been a thirteen fox forward observer, so he had some experience."

Major Kurt Merseal

"I used to get pissed and lobby and fight to get the supplies for the ANA. I would go directly to the minister of defense. I was just trying to get these soldiers clothes and just basic essentials that they needed. I would have to go to that level to get supplies, and it didn't take me long to figure out that the shit was there; the soldiers just really didn't want to have it. The Afghan government was not as ambitious about this eradication effort as what we were, and it was frustrating because you kind of think, well, these incompetent bastards at all levels, but they were brilliant in a sense that they had it figured out—they knew exactly what they were doing. It was passive resistance. It was tough on the Afghan officers because they were having so much political pressure put on them. Just another challenge we had to deal with.

"U.S. mentors at the top would want me to count weapons, they'd want me to be accountable and they would want me to just command the Afghans, but I refused to do it. I took some real beating over it, and my approach drew quite a bit of attention. I would go to a meeting, and the uppers knew not to ask me to go tell the Afghans what to do. Some of the other mentors began picking up on my approach, and they quit telling the Afghans what to do and just started mentoring them."

First Lieutenant Adam Cole

"The training continued with classes and PT, and then one day Lieutenant Williams was sent to pick up a new medic who was being assigned to the unit. The medic was at Camp Phoenix, which was on the other side of Kabul. We went to pick this kid up, and I was gunning on the way back, and he was going on and on about his girlfriend and he was glad that he'd be going out on missions but he was still close enough to go visit his girlfriend at Camp Phoenix. I was like, 'Where the hell do you think we are going?' and he's like 'Well, we're going to Camp Dubs, right?' I was like 'No, no, we're going to Helmand Province—you know, the place in the news where all the Marines are dying right now.' Then I said that where you are going and the NCO that assigned you will take care of your girlfriend. My buddy Willy who was with me tore into me and told me to knock it off. I did."

Major Kurt Merseal

In addition to shaping up the Afghan soldiers, Major Merseal had another issue: DynCorp.

"Our job was to go in and secure and area with the Afghan National Army, and then the DynCorp unit would come in with their tractors and four wheelers and mow the poppy down. The DynCorp workers were the Afghan police and were considered as elite almost just as the Kandak was considered to be. They were very well resourced and funded and had a lot of mentors, mostly American, and the unit was run through a DynCorp contract, which was run by Americans. They had spent $700 million over several years with this unit. The unit would be run by retired colonels or retired special forces guys. They were civilians, and there was no command structure by U.S. standards. They had no control over my unit, but they wanted to tell me what to do. The problem was all they were worried about was keeping their contracts, and the more poppy they eradicated, the more secure their contracts. They wanted to get stupid with missions and put my unit at risk. I wouldn't listen to them and wouldn't do what they said. They called the defense minister and told their story often, but I was able to say no to him and my generals stood behind me."

For several months there was training, frustration, and passive resistance with the ANA and the Afghan government. Not all frustration came from the training—some of it stemmed from a condition that always occurs when soldiers are sent into a new environment:

The Afghanistan Poppy Eradication Campaign

diarrhea. It was not a question of would people get it—the only question was *when*. Freddy Falmier had it. He was training with the ANA, and it hit him. He needed to get back to the camp in a hurry, so he ran for a Humvee and took off. There were some speed bumps on the road to the camp just down the road, and he had to go over each speed bump slowly, since the shocks on the Humvee didn't give very much. At about the third speed bump, his boots bloused and both legs and his pants were full. Cursing, he drove the rest of the way back.

He got out of the truck, went into the shower tent, and stripped down and took a shower. His living tent was about seventy-five yards from the shower tent. When he was done, he looked across the open area from the shower to his tent. "Fuck it!" And he walked to his tent with boots in hand and totally nude to get fresh clothes.

One of the things that also happens when men serve together in a foreign country, living together and fighting together, is that team members learn the others' personalities extremely well. One result of that familiarity is often nicknames, which was certainly true for the Black Hawk team. Major Kurt Merseal became BBK (By the Book), while Captain Greg Settle grew a dirty-looking mustache and was known as "Dirty Gary." Sergeant First Class Greg Settle was "Big Papa" because he was the ripe old age of 41; First Lieutenant. Adam Cole was "Ginger" because of his red hair; First Lieutenant Jason Williams was known as "Willy"; First Lieutenant William Sandell was "Snacks" because he always had his pockets full of crackers and candy bars; First Sergeant John Sury was known as "Storm" because of his temper; Staff Sergeant Freddy Falmier was "Skittles" because he liked the candy in the field rations; Sergeant First Class Jeffery Sowash was known as "Slow Wash" because of his name; and Staff Sergeant James Ressel wanted to be called James, so they called him Jimmy.

The Black Hawk team members had a tight bond; they had also trained the Afghanistan National Army (ANA) and built a working relationship with the Afghan soldiers.

Sergeant First Class Greg Strong

"The Afghanistan National Army is 80 percent illiterate, but they can see through the smokescreen. If you walk up, they can tell within

One • The Arrival

the first two minutes of a conversation if you are real or not. They will read you like a book, and they will play you the same way. We started training then and, hey, went along with it, but it's when you build the trust and we built that. We set up camp with them, and every morning we got up and trained, and they found out we were going with them on the missions. And you build and build the trust and then you have a group of soldiers that will fight with you. It is huge. I mean huge."

It was now time to move to Helmand Province to complete their mission of poppy eradication.

The night before they were due to leave, the ANA commander said they didn't have the necessary ammunition.

Major Kurt Merseal

"It wasn't because they couldn't get it; it was because they didn't really want to get it. All the influence and other ranking advisors were putting political pressure on them, but we met the challenge and got the ammo. The ANA soldiers had now realized that the American unit was going with them and began to build a trust with the Americans. The next stop, Helmand Province."

Helmand Province, January 2009

There were two feet of snow. The wind would cut into you in these tall mountains of Afghanistan. The one thing the troops could look forward to was a little warmer weather, since Helmand was at a lower elevation, but then they also had to deal with the Taliban.

First Lieutenant Adam Cole

"We were trying to get our trucks ready so as poppy season hit we could move south to Helmand. We were going in two giant convoys, and Afghanistan is the size of Texas, maybe a little bigger, and we had to drive across all of it pretty much, and in addition we had our ANA, who were spread all over hell, and then we had DynCorp, the Afghan

The Afghanistan Poppy Eradication Campaign

police, and all the shit that was being hauled with them, so it was literally like 120-vehicle convoy headed down Highway 1. There is one highway, and Major Merseal headed up the first convoy. Captain Settle was to head up the second convoy. Right before we were getting ready to go, we took our trucks in, got them checked over one last time, and on the way back through Kabul, I don't know what Mays was doing or how it happened, but he high centered a truck on this concrete barrier, and when he did we had to take the truck back in. They pulled my truck, which was all set up and Bill Brewer had spent hours just putting cup holders in there—I mean, he babied that truck like you wouldn't believe. They pulled that truck and our truck to go with the first convoy because they had to leave the next day. I had to take the truck back in to get it fixed and find a way to get back to Camp Dubs so we could go with the second convoy."

Major Merseal led the first convoy over the mountains and into Helmand Province. The journey took three days, with the troops stopping at assigned FOBs (Forward Observation Bases) along the way. On the third day, they arrived in the desert, away from everyone.

Major Kurt Merseal

"The first night that we rolled in, the colonel from DynCorp started trying to command and direct me. He started telling my guys how to mentor and what to do. It came that fast and came to a head right there. He told me that I would do what he told me to do or he would go to the ambassador, and when he did I would do what he told me, whether I wanted to or not. He did end up going and twisted his story to benefit him, but it didn't work. I stood my ground and I won. We would mentor and the Afghans would do the missions instead of us just telling them what to do and doing all the tasks ourselves."

The convoy stopped out in the middle of the desert, picked a spot, and started building a FOB to be known as FOB Eagle.[1] The weather was warmer, but there was still snow, cold, and a lot of mud. The new FOB would be set up with a circular perimeter. The ANA soldiers would secure half of the perimeter from 12 o'clock to 6 o'clock. The DynCorp National Police would cover the other half of the perimeter from 6 o'clock to 12 o'clock. The American team would mentor the line. Now the troops began to construct the cheesecloth tents in the center of the perimeter.

Captain Greg Settle

"We broke the team down basically into two groups, convoy one and convoy two. I had in charge of convoy two, and it took us three days to get to Helmand. I was to leave about a week after the first convoy left. We headed down, and it was an experience in itself, traveling across the country where you don't know anyone and you really don't know where you're going on top of the threat. It was a good long, hard ride, but we finally get down there, and we hadn't been in there probably ten minutes and we got attacked. We had a jingle truck [ANA truck] that got stuck in the mud. We had to pull security all night. We started receiving small arms incoming fire, but it didn't last but a few minutes. Then things settled down. In the middle of the night we could see some headlights coming across the desert, and that was when everything kind of started to set in as to how serious this was. I'd been in combat before in Iraq in 2005, but for some reason it was just different here. I was in Iraq and we did convoy security, but what we did was 99 percent during the day. This is the middle of the night, it's about 3 in the morning, and we have vehicles coming in, and we don't know who they are, and we got some light on them and found out that it was a Blue Ford tractor and not the enemy. A lot of my guys had never been in a fire fight before, so I told them, 'Well, boys, you got your cherry busted. Put your gear on and we will call it good and head down.'

"A few hours later the convoy arrived at the new FOB. It's the rainy season. The rain is pouring, sometimes in big drops and sometimes in small drops. It rains sideways and at times seems to even rain up. One of the worse rain storms in decades in Helmand Province.

"Our living conditions were horrible. We really didn't have much security. We were basically just out in the middle of the desert to put a stake in the ground, say this is home base. Built up some berms around it and had the Afghan National Army securing one side and the Afghan National Police securing the other side. We had to pull our own security, so I had to have one of my team members up at any given time. I remember after we were down there a few weeks we were tired,

The Afghanistan Poppy Eradication Campaign

really tired, because we didn't live in a FOB—we lived in the middle of the desert."

Sergeant First Class Greg Strong

"They issued cheesecloth tents. We had tents for us to live in and a tent for a chow hall. They were not waterproof; some had holes in them. They would stretch out, and we would have to use two by fours or tent poles to hold the roof up. We would have to make tarps to put over the top to get the rain to run off. It was horrible. We were just living in the middle of the desert with leaky tents and muddy floors. We ended up taking pallets and making our own floor.

"There was no American support for food; it was all brought in by TCN's Third World Nationals. They contracted them, and they were locals that run a catering business. The TCN served a lot of curry with bone still in, chicken curry with the bone, and rice. They also got lamb, which was one bite per lamp chop and tough as shoe leather. On occa-

FOB Eagle—cheesecloth tents to the left (photograph by Greg Strong).

sion the troops were ecstatic to get tater tots, French fries or little pizzas. We prayed for any American food we could get.

"It wasn't long before all the men began to lose weight. Later, when we started our missions, we'd laugh because during chow DynCorp would eat with us. We would be talking about fire fights, and they would then come up with their stories about being in fire fights. All they did was eradicate, but they can tell their story the way they want. That came later, though.

"Coupled with atrocious living quarters, constant rain, mud, cold weather, and food, there were no showers. Baby wipes were used for hygiene. In addition, no heads (bathrooms). When you had to go, you walked out into the desert and took a leak or dug a hole if you had to take a dump. We did come up with one seat for taking a dump. We had a folding chair and cut the seat out of it and wired a makeshift toilet seat to it. We called it the 'Decision Maker.' To say the least, it was 'Welcome to Helmand Province!'"

First Lieutenant Adam Cole

"We started building our FOB and getting everything ready to go out and actually start eradicating poppy, but before we did that we had to make a trip into an area call Lashkar Gah, which was a city in Helmand Province, and pick up a bunch of tractors for the Afghan soldiers to use to actually eradicate the poppy. That was one of our first real tasks because Lashkar Gah was a very non-secure area. There were coalition forces in the area, but it was one of the hot spots.

"My vehicle was the first vehicle, and I was driving that day. Normally I gun, but I was driving, and it was one of those days where everything just starts compounding. We get into the town, and we were driving down these narrow roads, and people are everywhere watching us. I turned the corner, and I'd like to say that the road gave out underneath me and I just started sliding into a ditch. My first reaction was to hammer it, get past where the problem was, and all that ended up doing was driving us further down into the canal. Major Merseal was behind us, and all he could see was the big antenna from our warlock system go over and disappear. For about the next two or three hours we had to deal with getting my Cougar out of the canal. I remember

The Afghanistan Poppy Eradication Campaign

MRAP Cougar stuck on the way to get tractors for eradication (photograph by Greg Strong).

thinking the whole time 'Major Merseal is just going to yell at me up and down.' He was not normally that type of guy, but I was thinking he was going to be very mad. He came up and assessed the situation. I remember it was a while before he said anything. We didn't roll all the way over; we were just sitting on the side. It was five or six minutes, we just sat there in silence, just trying to figure out what to do. We called in another vehicle and pulled the Cougar out.

"About three hours later we start out again, and we head down this stretch of road, I would say was about a half mile long, and there was literally six inches to clear from a wall on one side and a drop off into a much larger canal that I had already been in on the other. I had six inches. I don't mean six inches on either side; I had six inches of play for the whole vehicle. As we were going down it, it was muddy, and all I could do was barely turn the wheel and inch forward, and as

One • The Arrival

I inched forward the front wheel of the vehicle would slip right back into the edge of that ridge. About a quarter way through, we decided that everyone needed to get out of the vehicles; every bit of weight off the vehicles would help. I don't know how much the vehicle weighs, but at least ten tons. It took another hour for us to get a half mile. My lieutenant is ground guiding me, and Major Merseal is out and he keeps telling me he can see the mud on the canal side cracking each time I go through there. His concern wasn't the concern for my vehicle—there were two other vehicles behind me that had to come through behind me. If we had fallen off into the canal, it was a deep water canal and would have flipped us over, and we would never have been able to get the doors open. That was the scariest thing I had to go through.

"We got to the location where the tractors were and spent the night. We decided we needed to go around a different direction the next day."

Major Kurt Merseal

"We had to go to Lashkar Gah to pick up tractors for the eradication. Well, we could either drive all away around, four or five hours, or we could cut through the town of Nad Ali, and it was much shorter to go that route. I hadn't been through the town, but the people we had on ground told me our trucks would fit through the canals. Well, it had been raining and everything was muddy. They say we can do it, so we will do it. We were taking our big trucks, the MRAP Cougars, and we get there. These areas are real small, and we get into this town, and one of the trucks ahead of me gets stuck. I could just see it rolling over into the canal. All I could see was the antennas. I really couldn't see the truck. I see the antennas roll, and my heart just dropped. I knew they weren't hurt, but I knew the truck was really stuck bad. What had happened was Jimmy Ressel and Jeff Sowash was driving, and they turned the corner getting too close to it and it gave way. There was only one telephone pole in town, and it was there and caught the truck and kept it from completely turning over. It kept it halfway upright. We were able to wench it out with a couple other trucks.

"We had to drive on this narrow canal road at this point because we were too far into the town to turn around, so we had to go forward.

The Afghanistan Poppy Eradication Campaign

The roads were narrow, slick, and just horrible. We would take shovels and we would dig into the side of the back to try to get some traction to get a wheel like hooked in a rut so it would slide down the bank.

"The narrow roads had a big tall bank on the left side and there was a deep water canal right there, and it was like, if one of those trucks goes in that canal, there would be no way it is coming out, and then the crew is going to die because they would not be able to get the doors open, which were about 500 pounds each.

"I made everyone get out of the trucks except the driver. It was like 'Sorry drivers, but someone has to drive these damn things. There is no need for everyone to die if a truck rolls in the canal.' We were digging in the best we could, and we needed to get through because we had some Afghan police that had been hit in a fire fight, and we needed to get them help.

"What was nuts is I was holding the back bumper of a 20-ton truck trying to keep it from sliding in the ditch. I wasn't doing a damn thing to help, but I had to do something and the first truck had made it through. The first truck had cracked the road where it's sloping down in the canal. As my truck was inching forward, you would see the cracks forming on the side slope of the road. The driver would go about a foot, and the truck would slide down a bit. He would turn the wheels the other direction and go another foot. It was like a dead man walking watching him drive that truck. We finally got all the trucks through without any trucks turning over.

"We went the long way around going back. It put us a day or two behind, but it was well worth it."

The Black Hawk team returned to FOB Eagle with the tractors and equipment. The team tried to relax after the gut-wrenching experience of crossing the narrow canals. They ate their rations, battled the cold and mud, used baby wipes to do their best to stay clean, and dug holes or used the "Decision Maker" to relieve themselves, but it was early spring and the poppy was starting to sprout. The focus now switched; it was time for the first mission.

Two

The Ambush

> "I was leaving Fort Riley and I get a call from Kurt Merseal, the team chief. He says, 'Have you heard of Helmand Province?' I said, 'No, I guess I better Google it.' He says, 'Have you ever heard of a team called CNIK?' 'CNIK?' 'Yeah, Counter Narcotics Infantry Kandak.' We did some research, and one of the first things I read was that Helmand Province was the best place to give your life for your country. I read on and said, 'Holy cow, this could get interesting, this could get real very fast.'"—Captain Greg Settle

February 1, 2009—North of Nad Ali City

It was cold and there was a dampness in the air, but, fortunately for the Black Hawk team, it wasn't raining. The weather wasn't their concern on this day, though—it was the mission, their first mission. They were moving about, loading the trucks, checking the weapons, loading ammunition, and trying to organize the Afghanistan National Army (ANA). The situation was surreal, and it was hard to believe that they were about to go into possible combat. On their minds, although none spoke about it, was the Oregon National Narcotics team that had lost half of its men doing exactly what the Black Hawk team was about to encounter. Finally, the trucks were lined up with the Black Hawk team, the ANA, and DynCorp, with tractors and equipment to eradication the poppy. It was time to move out.

The plan was for ANA's Counter Narcotics Infantry Kandak (CNIK) to conduct a joint operation with DynCorp in and north of Nad Ali on the near side of the canal in February 2009. The CNIK exe-

The Afghanistan Poppy Eradication Campaign

cuted its task by establishing the outer cordon through a series of screen lines and blocking positions around target area 4 for eradication. The screen lines would be along Cos Yellow 4 and 2 in the south, along Yellow lines 4 and 15 grid in the east, and along the 20 grid line in the west, and they would initially provide a company along the northeastern and western screen lines. THE CNIK commander's intent was to safely conduct a tactical move from FOB Dylan V to the assigned eradication area NET. 1st Advising Team (War Pig), 2nd Advising Team (Thumper), and HQ Advising Team (Redman) would move with the force for support. A British contingent would also move with the force for additional support and travel in one of the M-1151s to provide further protection.[1]

Once passing the release point, the 1st and 2nd Advising Teams began moving along the eastern portion of the screen line to get into position.

MRAP Cougar Redman at Nad Ali over-watch (photograph by Greg Strong).

Two • The Ambush

Sergeant First Class Jeffery Sowash

"My vehicle was usually the lead vehicle, but this time we weren't the lead. We were trying to cross this area, and when the snow melts it runs down and creates a very soft sand area. The first truck got stuck and was trying to figure out what they were going to do, and so we went down further south trying to find a place to cross, and we found a hard-packed road which looked like a place where all the Afghans had been taking their carts. Now I am the lead vehicle, and we get across the wade, which is a few hundred feet wide. I was on the gun. As we neared the southernmost post of the screen line, we began receiving direct small arms, machine-gun fire, and indirect (mortar and RPG) fire. I heard something behind me, and I turned around, and there was a smoke screen coming at me, and I kind of ducked and it went right over my hood, and whatever it was—a mortar or rocket—it just barely missed me and blew up about 20 meters from the vehicle. Right after that everything opened up. There was small arms fire, RPGs, mortars were coming in, and we couldn't turn around. There were Afghans between me and Major Merseal, but his was the next mentor truck. Staff Sergeant Ressel maneuvered the truck into a position about 50 meters to the south, to allow for a clearer line of fire. I'm trying to get my gun turned and opened up on them with the .50 caliber, and at the same time mortars were coming in and hitting all around the truck. There is all kinds of small arms fire coming in, and I continued to return fire with the 50. I looked over to see why the Afghan soldiers weren't returning fire. They had all left their vehicles and were hiding behind some dirt mounds 75 meters or so from where their trucks were located. One ANA soldier was wounded by shrapnel in the shoulder."

A few minutes later, the 3rd Advising Team (First Lieutenant William Sandell, Sergeant First Class Jeffery Sowash, Staff Sergeant James Ressel, Private First Class Michael Garcia, and interpreter Mahammad Noor), traveling in Wizard, crossed over the release point and began to receive direct small arms and machine-gun fire and indirect mortar and RPG fire to the east of the riverbed. Major Kurt Merseal, Sergeant First Class Sean Rabbitt, Staff Sergeant Kyle Campbell, Specialist Nathaniel Rowton, and interpreter Mirab were to the

The Afghanistan Poppy Eradication Campaign

rear of Wizard across the riverbed at the time.[2] Staff Sergeant Campbell began to return fire with the MK-19 as well.

Staff Sergeant Kyle Campbell

"We were moving into the area, and everything just got loud. Everything was coming fast. I don't know how many places we were taking fire from, but we had walked into an ambush. I saw the Taliban shooting at us from some buildings, and I was on the Mark 19—it fires the grenades. It's a slow-traveling grenade before it hits, so there's time of flight that takes place. And there was this guy, he would kind of pop out around the corner and shoot at us, and then I would shoot back at him, but by the time the grenade could get to him he'd already ducked away. Major Merseal pointed to a spot next to a building and told me to shoot at that spot. I didn't see anything there, but I fired about a 5-round burst, and I can see a Taliban guy jump up and run behind cover. I don't know if it was just pure luck on that guy's part or what, but it was incredibly frustrating to see that happen.

"I could see them behind a wall. I couldn't see the mortar, but I could see the flashes and the smoke come above the wall, and then the mortars landing around all over our position and around the Afghans and national police. We were in the riverbed and probably shouldn't have been, but it was our first mission and sometimes you make mistakes. I just elevated the Mark 19 so that I could get the grenades to skip right over the top of the wall and right in where the war team was, and once I did I didn't see any more flashes from the mortar. The enemy fire was sporadic and ineffective, as they were effectively suppressed by concealment of a building. The enemy used doorways and small holes to conceal their fire."

First Lieutenant Brian Mays

"We started taking fire, and that was the first time I had been in combat, and I remember standing at the back of the truck and I looked over to my left at Greg Settle, and we just kind of looked at each other, and I was 'WOW, this is happening.' I was scared, but at the same time I was kind of excited because I was like, this is what it feels like to be shot at and to hear the rounds whizzing past your ears. It just took you to a whole new place, and I connected with Settle, and he said, 'Go ahead and start returning fire.' I lit them up."

First Lieutenant Adam Cole

"We had started seeing some IEDs as we were going down there; they were putting them blown up form on the edges of the roads and fields. They were trying to canalize us, but nothing too bad. We were going to go in on one movement, and then we were going to split off and go down two forks and establish security. Sandell was going to go down one of them, and Settle was going to go down the other. Merseal was going to stick with Sandell.

"Sandell got lost, and apparently it was a good thing because the route he was going to take had IEDs all over it, and DynCorp ended up getting one of their trucks blown up by an IED on that same route. I wasn't there for all of it, but Sandell ended up having to help an ANA soldier who got shot in the balls, and then we all made jokes about him fondling the ANA soldier. There was a big ass fight going on over there.

"Settle and I just started pushing down, Settle up further from me, and I see him just start getting lit up. I see them shooting from over here, and there's mortar rounds impacting, and he had hit the point that they were in range of all the weapons systems. We had stopped our truck—me, Freddy, and Willy—just short of there. We were sitting there firing on the Taliban, and Merseal tells Settle to go ahead and pull back, DynCorp is not going down that far, it's too high.

"He pulls back, leaves me down there sitting, and Merseal is trying to figure out how to go ahead and establish the rest of that security and lock in our perimeter. Well, he decides he is going to send Sandell down, and there's like one good route down there. We were sitting on it, and we were right at the edge and just out of the Taliban's range. Sandell comes down, and I hop out of my truck and I go over, and I was like 'Hey, you push any further south, and they are going to light you up with mortars. They are fucking waiting on us.'

"Merseal wants us to get further down, and the only way we can get there is on this route, and we are going to take fire if we do it. They drive up about another ten meters, and we started getting mortared and they start lighting us up. I was starting to get confident with getting

The Afghanistan Poppy Eradication Campaign

shot at because I was dumb, and I am doing my little John Wayne walk around, getting the ANA set up. Freddy is out there with me. I think we had Tyminsky in the truck, and that's how we had Freddy able to move around, and while this whole thing is going on, I am trying to get Sandell's guys to maneuver too.

"He's still in his truck, and I'm like 'Freddy, keep these guys moving. Get them set up along these buildings,' and I had to get Sandell out of his truck. I go over to Sandell's truck because his guys had snatched up some old man and they were just beating the shit out of him, and I didn't know if he was actually an insurgent or not. It was pretty early, us being down there, and they are just beating the shit out of him, and I was like 'hell, they got him, and he is disarmed if he had a weapon, no reason to beat the shit out of him.'

"I tried to get them to stop, so I decided I would just go get Sandell. I get to the truck and beat on the door, and he opens it, and I tell him to get the fuck out of the truck, his guys are beating the piss out of some old man. Sandell kind of hesitates and then gets out, and Garcia gets out with him. Garcia's eyes are about the size of a silver dollar, and he is looking all over the place, and I said, 'Don't worry, we aren't going to get shot at right here,' and about that time a couple rounds cracked right over my head.

"We hit the dirt, and I am getting as close to the ground as I can get, saying, 'Oh, shit.' Garcia is with me, and his eyes are still big as silver dollars. Meanwhile, Freddy is still trying to maneuver our guys all over hell and just having a good old time with his M-19 and lighting everything up, and they finally stop shooting.

"I get over there with Sandell, and they had finally stopped beating the old man. They are sitting there with him and trying to figure out what was going on. I asked Sandell if he was OK. He said he was good and went back over to check on Freddy. I started running back over, and most of the firing was up and to our left, and that's where Freddy was maneuvering our guys.

"I was like 'Garcia, what the fuck you doing?' He said, 'There's a guy, he keeps peeking his head around the corner.' I was like 'Which way are we getting shot at from?' He says, 'Well, from over there,' pointing. I was like 'OK, where are the ANA?' He yells, 'Over there,' where

Two • The Ambush

he said the shooting was coming from, and he fired a couple more rounds. I am pretty confident he didn't do it, but there was an ANA soldier that had taken a round in the shoulder.

"I was like 'Oh, shit,' but I don't think that Garcia actually shot him. It was just another string of the shit show that day. It was really a hot one that day."

First Lieutenant Troy Kemper

"It was really an eye opener that, hey, they are shooting at us and we are shooting back. They are really trying to kill us and we are trying to kill them. I was the gunner in Major Merseal's Cougar, and we were at an outpost on the perimeter. We start seeing locals moving into a particular building, and then the Taliban opened up on us from another area. They are firing RPGs small arms fire and mortars. I am firing back with the .50 caliber, and First Sergeant Sury is on the ground firing AT4s at the buildings. Then, about three ammo cans into the fire fight, it stopped. It was the first that I had been in battle, and although it was happening, it was hard to wrap my head around."

As the CNIK team continued to suppress the enemy fire, a DynCorp truck backed into an IED, which completely destroyed the truck.

First Lieutenant Troy Kemper

"I remember we were hollering over the radio, trying to get everyone to move in the right direction, get suppressing fire, and the state trackers were behind us and there was a big explosion. It was one of the Afghan trucks, and I remember hearing the explosion, and I look and it is just up in the air and then slammed down, black smoke everywhere. I was thinking to myself, 'There is no way those guys are going to live.' As soon as it hit, the driver and the passenger both got out and started running from the vehicle unscathed. I couldn't believe it."

As the fire fight continued, two CNIK soldiers were hit—one in the thumb and the other in the groin. First Lieutenant Sandell and Private First Class Garcia exited their vehicle while under fire and ran approximately 25 meters behind a mound of dirt for cover to aid the second wounded soldier. The team medic, Specialist Rowton, then ran to the scene to assess the wounds and provide combat care under fire

The Afghanistan Poppy Eradication Campaign

until the soldier could be transported out of the immediate area. The 3rd Advising Team attempted to secure transportation for the wounded soldier through an ANA soldier nearby, but the soldier would not leave his covered position because there was heavy machine-gun fire. Private Garcia, disregarding his own safety and acting on his own initiative, took off running under heavy fire, with machine-gun rounds kicking up dirt all around him and over his head. He opened the door of an ANA truck and jumped in as bullets glanced off the vehicle. He got it started as a mirror was shattered on the driver's side.

While Garcia was maneuvering the truck, First Lieutenant Sandell, with his pockets stuffed full of crackers and candy bars, was applying pressure the wounded ANA soldier's injury to stop the bleeding. A rain of fire was moving in both directions, from the ANA soldiers and Black Hawks to the Taliban and back again. Even though there was heavy fire, members of the Black Hawk team were yelling at Lieutenant Sandell, giving him grief because he was holding the ANA soldier's groin. Finally, Garcia maneuvered the truck to their position to provide cover and then transport the wounded ANA soldier away.

Staff Sergeant Kyle Campbell

"Lieutenant Sandell was over there doing everything he could to keep restriction so there wasn't as much blood loss. I remember the medic wanting us to back the truck up to where the wounded were, and we're all screaming to just do his job; we weren't going to back up there, it was chaotic. It was somewhat entertaining, though, but sometimes you just have to find humor. Lieutenant Sandell was holding this guy's nut sack. I don't know if it was lifesaving, but we all gave him a lot of hell for putting his hands on the Afghan's nut sack. I would want someone to help me, but it was just humorous. All the guys got razzed about something.

"Then, while we are still trying to get everyone out of there, Private First Class Garcia, with lead coming at him from everywhere, started running out from the defilade, grabbing a Afghan truck and driving it to the wounded. I just couldn't believe he was running through all that small arms fire, RPGs and mortar rounds, but he did because no one else would do it. Lieutenant Sandell was with him, but he didn't have to say a word to Garcia. Garcia saw what he had to do and did it.

"Meanwhile, the ANA was laying down small arms fire, I am on the 50 laying down fire, and Kyle Campbell is in the gunner turret in Major Merseal's truck and he is laying down Mark 19 and 240 rounds everywhere. We finally move out of that area and move down where the other guys are, and their fire fight had calmed down somewhat. We laid the screen line so the Afghan National Police could eradicate the poppy. We started receiving more machine-gun fire and RPGs and mortar fire. We answered with Mark 19s, 240 rounds and .50 caliber rounds. The Afghan National Police are stuck in the mud and trying to get out. Another fire fight breaks out, and we are laying down fire once again. They get the trucks unstuck and move in position to eradicate the poppy, and another fire fight breaks loose. I remember thinking to myself, 'There's no way I'm going to survive this; it may not be today, it may not be tomorrow, but if I'm down here for three months, there's no way I'm going to get that lucky this whole time.'"

Another ANA soldier was wounded, so Major Merseal requested a 9-line medevac because he needed immediate care. The machine-gun fire and RPGs were still coming in heavy, and the Black Hawk team was returning fire with the .50 calibers and M-19s. The ANA soldiers were returning fire at a rapid rate as the medevac helicopters arrived. The wounded soldiers were loaded on cots, and team members ran toward the helicopters with dirt flying up all around them as they loaded the wounded on board. The helicopters lifted and made a hard right in the air, heading for Camp Bastion.

Then Major Merseal decided that the best action was to withdraw from the area and call in close air support to suppress the enemy fire. It was obvious that the thick walls built around the clots that the Taliban fighters were hiding behind would be difficult to penetrate even with the .50 calibers. The force withdrew approximately one kilometer to the north. Two Marine Apache helicopters came in firing rockets and machine guns on the clots. When they did, the firing from the Taliban stopped.

At that time, a request was logged for an emergency resupply of

The Afghanistan Poppy Eradication Campaign

ammunition for the CNIK, since the ammunition status was amber (low on ammunition) and approaching red (almost out of ammunition). The Diablo element (Department of State Air Wing helicopter) left the FOB with the emergency supply of ammunition for CNIK. Since the helicopter had weight limits, the priority ammunition (AK-47 rounds, DSHKs, PKMs, and RPGs) was shipped and arrived in a short time.[3]

DynCorp concluded its eradication operation, and the screen line was collapsed. While moving back into the riverbed, the 2nd and 3rd Advising Teams were again engaged in a fire fight. The Taliban sent a rain of machine-gun fire and RPGs at the Black Hawk team. They answered with the M-19s, 240 rounds, and .50 caliber rounds. One ANA soldier was hit in the helmet by small arms fire but was uninjured. After an hour of fighting, the enemy ceased to fire as the units moved back to the FOB. DynCorp estimated the amount of poppy eradicated for the day at 51.72 hectares (1 hectare equals 2.4 acres).[4] The Black Hawk team had spent five and a half hours involved in fire fights while DynCorp eradicated the poppy.

On the return journey to the FOB, the CNIK engaged a motorcycle as it neared the FOB site area. Concerned about a possible suicide bombing, they fired warning shots over the motorcycle. The motorcycle stopped, quickly turned around, and drove off. A short time later the Black Hawks pulled into FOB Eagle.

Sergeant First Class Jeffery Sowash

"We checked our vehicles, and I can remember taking pictures of all the bullet dings that were on our vehicle, and they were everywhere on the vehicle. I don't want to make it sound like there were hundreds of them, but there were at least 50 dings. A blast from an IED had left a ridge in one place on the Cougar. I knew one thing: I had been lucky. I went to my cheesecloth tent. They call them South African summer tents. They are made for warm weather. It was freezing cold, and the corners of the tent didn't even come together. It was sloppy with mud, and we had pallets to put our gear on; otherwise it would be sitting in the mud. I made a fire pit in the middle of my tent and burned charcoal to stay warm. Major Merseal came in and told me I couldn't burn charcoal in the tent because I could die from carbon monoxide poisoning.

Two • The Ambush

At the same time he sat down next to the charcoal fire and warmed himself up. I'm thinking to myself, 'I got four-foot caps in the corners of my tent, I'm not too worried about carbon monoxide.'"

The men went to the chow tent for food. All were starved after a day of fighting. The locals had grilled lamb chops; there was also rice with something mixed in it. Sergeant First Class Greg Strong dropped two of the chops on his plate. They were so small that there was only one bite per chop, but that was all right. The chops would last a long time because they were as tough as a combat boot heel, and they tasted about the same. The only thing that was good was the cold drinks of water and soda.

The men ate and returned to their cheesecloth tents, walking on the wooden pallets to stay out of the mud. They attempted to decompress as much as was possible in a war zone and prepared for a night of sleep. Sleep was important because the next day would be another mission of eradicating poppy and fighting. The Black Hawk CNIK 16-man team had completed its first mission successfully. In five hours of continuous fire fights, thousands of rounds expended, and thousands of rounds, RPGs, and mortars received, the poppy eradication had not stopped once. Yet they had returned to the FOB as a team unscathed. Now they fought the cold and the mud, using baby wipes and eating their field rations, but for sure God was with them because they had a folding chair with a toilet seat wired to it, the "Decision Maker."

Three

Afghanistan National Army Two KIAs

"I was put in for a Bronze Star with Valor, but I don't need to broadcast it. It was a moment in time that I look back at and am very grateful for what I went through. It definitely helped me develop more responsibly as a young man."—Lieutenant Brian Mays"

February 16, 2009

The Black Hawk team members were up early, preparing for another mission. They were loading trucks, checking their weapons and loading ammunition, a task that had now become a daily routine. It was a routine of prepare for a mission, fight, and sleep, coupled with minimal meals and baby wipes for a shower, day after day, while DynCorp eradicated the poppy. This mission would be north of Nad Ali City.

The operation was to be conducted over a two-day period, operating from a patrol base north of Nad Ali City on the near side of the canal. The CNIK was to execute its task by establishing the outer perimeter through a series of screen lines and blocking positions around target area 16, with 16A being an alternate. For eradication, the area would be 18 grid line to the north, along 23 grid line to the east, then along 16 grid line to the south and initially along 23 grid line to ultimately end along the 20 grid line to the west. The commander was to conduct a tactical move from the patrol base to the assigned erad-

Three • Afghanistan National Army Two KIAs

ication area. The order of march would be 3rd Advising Team (Wizard), HQ Advising Team (Redman), 1st Advising Team (War Pig) and then 2nd Advising Team (Thumper). A British contingent would also move out for additional support, traveling in one of the M-1151s to provide more force protection than the team's vehicles could provide. The plan was that the units were to position themselves based on the scheme of the maneuver that the Kandak commander developed.

The 1st Advising Team included Captain Greg Settle, First Lieutenant Brian Mays, and Sergeant First Class Greg Strong, with Ramin Barack Darokhan and Mustafa Noori assigned as interpreters. The 2nd Advising Team included Captain Mark Foth, First Lieutenant Adam Cole, First Lieutenant Jason Williams, Staff Sergeant Freddy Falmier, and Captain Anthony McLean, with Haroom Ahmed as interpreter. The 3rd Advising Team included First Lieutenant William Sandell, Sergeant First Class Jeffery Sowash, Staff Sergeant James Ressel, and Private First Class Michael Garcia; Mahammad Noor was the interpreter assigned to the third team, which would travel in the Cougar Wizard.[1]

The convoy moved out. An hour into the convoy movement, one of the Black Hawk team members came over the radio: "We need to take five." Everyone knew what it meant—someone had to take a dump because of diarrhea. Just another part of life in the desert. A short time later the convoy moved out again. An hour later they were moving into the canal zone near the sector where they had been tasked with their mission.

The canal zones are more condensed and mobility is reduced, making convoys a more vulnerable target. The Taliban took advantage of this situation and began laying down small arms fire from the southeast of their position. A short time later an RPG7 warhead penetrated the window of one of first company's Ford Rangers, going through the front seat and lodging in the back seat. It didn't explode. DynCorp's Explosive Ordnance Team (EOD) was requested, as the warhead was still intact.

The EOD team usually consisted of two men. They would be called on to address all unexploded IEDs and bombs. In this case, they opened the doors of the truck, climbed into the back seat, carefully removed the unexploded warhead—as cool, calm, and collected as if they were

The Afghanistan Poppy Eradication Campaign

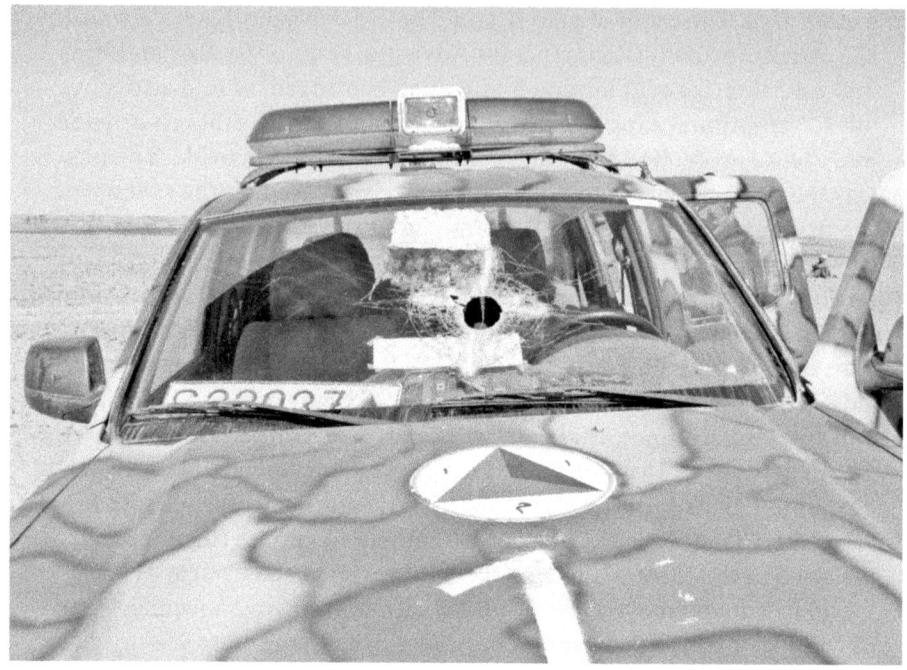

Afghan Ford truck hit by RPG (photograph by Greg Strong).

having a morning cup of coffee—from the back seat, placed it in their vehicle and drove away. Later, the EOD team detonated the warhead.

Major Kurt Merseal

"We were on the outskirts of Nad Ali, and we knew we were getting ready to go into a canal zone, and that makes things more condensed mobility wise and gave the Taliban the advantage at that point of the maneuver. The ability to fight was going to be critical. We dropped a couple compounds with hell fires, and the fight was raging intensely. An RPG came flying by mortar guy Sergeant Rabbitt. It missed him by feet and stuck in the Ford truck he was standing right beside of. It went through the front window and the driver's seat and lodged in the back seat, but thank God it didn't blow up, or Sergeant Rabbitt would have probably been killed, or at least seriously wounded."

Three • *Afghanistan National Army Two KIAs*

First Lieutenant Adam Cole

"We were driving out, and there was a big crowd of people trying to stop us. We were just trying to work our way through because as soon as they saw vehicles they would flood their poppy fields so that would canalize us to the roads, and once they canalized us to the roads it was easier to blow us up. I didn't know that then, I was just starting to figure it out, but this first time they got this big ass crowd of people and they start crowding around the truck and start throwing rocks. I got on the radio to my interpreter and told him to get the ANA out and move them away. I had this shitty company commander; he had just taken off and left. He wasn't even there. I was like 'The hell with it; I am going to get out and get us moving.' Willy was yelling at me and telling me not to get out of the truck; 'they will fucking kill you.' I yelled back and said, 'Well, if they do, then shoot them.'

"I hopped out of the truck and started talking to the guy who looked like he was in charge. I had practiced the language and had gotten pretty good at it working with the ANA and had enough to get by without an interpreter. I start talking to this guy and introducing myself. I tell him they need to move. My interpreter is there, sitting and looking at them and looking at me and just smiling and nodding his head. He says something back, and I was like 'I didn't catch,' so I looked at my interpreter and said, 'What the hell did he say?' 'He doesn't speak the language you're using,' the interpreter responded. I said, 'Thanks, will you fucking tell him what I am saying, then, so we get moved?' He told him, and we moved about ten feet, and they all came back, and I was like 'What the fuck is going on?' We keep trying to get the people moved. I'm getting my ANA out slowly to start pushing the people back.

"Settle's coming down another route, and he's got his ANA out now and they're moving up. About that time I hear shooting. I look to my left and the ANA are shooting. They aren't shooting at the crowd, so I'm looking and thinking, 'What the fuck they shooting at?' I look to my right, and Settle's ANA are shooting, and then I saw rounds coming right toward me. I run for the truck and get back in the truck and yelled, 'Everybody good? I'm back in.' Freddy yells at me and says, 'You

The Afghanistan Poppy Eradication Campaign

left Sowash outside.' I see him scratching at the door. I just pop it and grab him and pull him in.

"What I found out later was the insurgents had coerced the crowd into demonstrating against us because, I mean, they weren't happy we were screwing up their poppy fields. The insurgents were hoping we would fire into the crowd, and when we didn't they fired into the crowd. I ended up having to patch up this kid and talking to him. He had got gut shot, and his intestines were hanging out. Willy started freaking out, and I told him to just pull security and let me worry about the kid. He was about 8 years old, and his name was Askerod. We got Department of State medevac and the British helped coordinate it."

Sergeant First Class Jeffery Sowash

"They had stopped us in the road, and they were breaking our headlights out. Some of our people had brought the KC day lighters and had mounted them on their trucks so that we could get a little better illumination. The Afghans were breaking them off. They were throwing rocks at us and hitting the windshields. The rocks weren't coming through, but it was cracking the bulletproof glass on the windows. The Taliban opened up while the crowd was around our trucks. One kid got hit in the stomach. It isn't a pretty sight to look at, but I and the lieutenant got out and got him on a stretcher so the ANA could medevac him. We got back into the vehicle, rounds bouncing off the Cougar, and started moving into the village."

Staff Sergeant James Ressel

"I've never seen combat before and never been shot at before, but I remember I was gunning that day and we had gone to do some of the poppy fields. All the villagers came out, and they were lying down in front of the trucks and wouldn't let us go anywhere. They didn't want us to go into their poppy fields and destroy them. The next thing you know, someone opened up into the crowd of villagers and started shooting. It wasn't us, but at the time I thought it was the ANA, but it was the Taliban. RPGs are flying, and it was really scary. I said, 'Holy shit,' and just froze for about 5 or 6 seconds without doing anything. I didn't have a target and was trying to figure out what was happening. RPGs blowing up everywhere, and I made a conscious decision at that time I wasn't going to let fear or being scared of getting hurt or dying dominate what I did. It is what it is, and I was better in doing my job from that point forward."

First Lieutenant Adam Cole

"We were going on a mission, and the Taliban knew we were coming because about the time we got near the village about two hundred villagers came out. They were lying in the road, and we couldn't go anywhere. The ANA weren't doing anything, and we are at a standstill, and then people started shouting and throwing rocks. Lieutenant Williams says, 'I'm going to get out and talk to them.' I begged him not to get out of the truck, but he got out anyway. He goes and talks to them, and I am on the gun and trying to cover him. Major Merseal gets on the radio and says, 'Hey, we got intel that there's a guy in a white robe with a white turban. He's a suicide bomber. He is headed right toward you guys. Don't let him get near you.' Everybody's wearing white robes, and I'm like 'You're fucking kidding me.' About that time the ANA start trying to move these people out. A young ANA, I think he was a lieutenant, pulled his pistol out and started shooting in the ground. That just erupted everything. I mean, RPGs going up and shooting everywhere. I don't even know what they were shooting at, but the crowd started to scatter. When the dust settled a little, an older man had been shot in the leg and a kid had been shot in the stomach and his intestines were hanging out.

"After that I hated the Afghans because there was no reason to shoot that kid. We medevacked the kid and he was operated on, and they took a 5.45 round out of him, which is from a Russian-made round. The Taliban had shot the civilians to try to make it look like the ANA or our guys had shot into the crowd. They had no concern for human life."

The 1st and 3rd ANA companies began to receive small arms fire and machine-gun fire from a clot. They dismounted from the trucks and returned fire. The advising teams fired on several clots as the 2nd

The Afghanistan Poppy Eradication Campaign

Platoon, 1st Company ANA forces pushed forward to assault the enemy fighters located to their south.

The first house was cleared with little resistance. The platoon then began to receive fire from a clot to the east. Two platoons from the 2nd Company were ordered to move forward to support the 1st Company. Unfortunately, the executive officer of the company had turned his radio off, and the platoons failed to move in.

The 2nd Platoon, 1st Company approached the clot to the east. As two of the ANA soldiers came to the entrance of the clot, machine-gun fire erupted. One soldier was hit in the head and the other in the torso. At this time the 1st and 3rd advising teams were moving forward to the position. First Lieutenant Brian Mays pushed forward with his team and determined that one soldier was KIA. He then moved forward of their position and, under heavy machine-gun fire, threw a grenade into the house where the machine-gun fire was coming from. Immediately, the firing from the enemy stopped.

Major Kurt Merseal

"We started moving in to clear a compound. The Afghans took turns on who ran the show on combat operations. The colonel very seldom came out, so the executive officer pretty much ran the show. He was a great guy, and I trusted him with my life many times. He was a fighter, and we moved into this village, and we had an intense fire fight going on. He was in charge that day, and I was mentoring him to take significant force and start clearing a compound. They had send a platoon out, and I know Captain Settle and Lieutenant Mays had dismounted and moved forward. The operation turned into complete chaos because the Afghans didn't know how to maneuver. They were basically walking across this field and we were providing the support fire for them, and they got ahead of us and came around the compound and got chewed up. We lost two Afghan soldiers that day. I was the guy saying, 'Hey, you need to maneuver on these Taliban.' There was a little tension between us at that time, but I made sure I just mentored them. It was a redefining point that day because the Afghans thought they were really good in their minds, and we didn't think they were that good and that day confirmed it. A lesson learned."

Three • Afghanistan National Army Two KIAs

Lieutenant Brian Mays

"We got close to this town, and there were numerous little huts. They have these mud walls surrounding them, and they were called clots. As soon as we entered the town we started to take fire. We started to penetrate into the town and we let the ANA lead the sweep through, and then we would come behind and make sure they had done the sweep the way we taught them. As we were sweeping through we lost contact with the ANA first sergeant. I told Captain Settle that I was going to dismount and go up forward and find out what was going on. We were still taking fire and we didn't have contact with the ANA, which was a problem. Captain Settle said, 'Well, I am going with you.'

"Me and Settle took our interpreter with us and started moving forward. I remember our interpreter was behind us, and as we moved forward we were trying to determine where the fire was coming from. As we moved forward we located this small house where the fire was coming from, and the house was like half underground. It was almost like they were shooting from a basement. We had rounds popping in front of us and all around us, and I don't know how we kept from getting hit. We took cover in the next building we came to. The interpreter was talking with some of the ANA on the radio, and they told him that the first sergeant was killed and he was on the other side of the house where the small arms fire was coming from. We couldn't work around the building because the small arms fire was too heavy, so Captain Settle asked me if I had a grenade. I said, 'Yes, I have two of them.' He said, 'Give me one; I am going to drop it in that house.' I told him no, it was my grenade; I was going to do it. The Taliban was really putting out the small arms fire. He said, 'OK, I am going to provide support for you.' It felt like basic training just went right back into my head, and I just went through the motions of how I was trained. I started a low crawl toward the house, and Captain Settle was just laying the fire into that house. Major Merseal's truck is like right in front of me, and the .50 caliber is aimed right at this house. I crawled up, and there was this little burlap bag hanging over this opening. I lifted it up and tossed the grenade in. Three seconds later it exploded.

"The British unit moved up and started putting fire into a side

The Afghanistan Poppy Eradication Campaign

window while Captain Settle and me moved around to the back of the house. Sure enough, we found the first sergeant. His head was split open—I mean, brains hanging out of his skull and half of his face looked like hamburger. Captain Settle told me to help carry him, and we had to get him into a body bag. We started, but I ended up cradling him and I had his brains hanging on my arm, and I remember just think my mind to a different place and just acting, just do what you have to do. We got to this ledge, and then one of our trucks backed up and had a body bag ready. We laid him in it and zipped the bag up. We went back to the Cougar, and I looked at Captain Settle and thought, 'Wow, that just happened.'"

First Lieutenant Adam Cole

"We ended up setting up security, and we had had gone through the entire plan. We hit one spot one day and would hit another spot right next to it the next day. DynCorp decided they were going to set up on this hilltop that overlooked the entire area. They did that the first day, and then the next day they were talking about doing it again. Major Merseal told them that it was a bad idea. We went up there and three ANA were killed because they put IEDs all over that hilltop. I don't remember the guy's name, but he was a real asshole. He was a retired lieutenant colonel—just an arrogant cocksucker. He was trying to flank us. I don't think he was selected for promotion, and he was just bitter about it. Major Merseal said they were going to try to flank us, so he had asked me to set up on the western side with my company. We get set up, and sure enough they tried to flank us. DynCorp was taking the eastern side and they rolled on the eastern flank, and Major Merseal and Captain Settle was down there, and they took the brunt of it. We decided to try to maneuver on them, trying to clear houses. The insurgents were trying to get us to move on them because they had secondary positions set to hit us. After we got through the first row of houses, they just lit up on us. We had two ANA soldiers killed.

"I am just sitting there, bored out of my mind. We were getting bits and pieces of the fight, and we heard that there were wounded. We thought it was U.S. wounded. We take off hell in across these hills, I

Three • *Afghanistan National Army Two KIAs*

mean we were airborne, and we get down there and see Sergeant Rabbitt; I saw an RPG that had gone through the windshield, front seat of an ANA Ford truck and was stuck in the back seat of the cab. Sergeant Rabbitt is just standing right by the Ford truck, and I asked where the hell Captain Settle and the other guys were at. He pointed off in one direction, and we take off hell in again.

"We come to this big muddy field, and I told the driver not to take the truck across it. I got out and said, 'Come on, Doc, let's go,' and we are doing this big ass run across this wide open field, and I am thinking the whole time, 'We got to get across this field or we are going to get shot.' I looked back and the doc, who was a civilian nurse, wasn't in the best shape, had stopped and was sitting and just panting. I said, 'We got to get across this field; we are going to get our asses shot, come on.'

"The last I had heard from them on the radio they said they needed a bag. I thought they meant they needed an aid bag. We got over there, and the top of one guy's head was just gone and the other one had just been stitched up, and I think he took one in the head too. I was like 'Oh, you meant you needed a body bag.'"

The Taliban fighters continued using doorways and small holes to conceal their fire. The Black Hawk team strove to suppress the enemy fire but with minimal effect, as the team's weapons could not penetrate the structures: the walls were too thick. Attack Apache helicopters were called to the clot and, with two hellfire missiles and a 30mm machine-gun rocket, effectively destroyed it.

Fourteen detainees were captured by the ANA from the area as suspected Taliban.[2] Dressed in robes and head wraps, and with their hands placed on their heads, they were marched out of the village and transported back to FOB Eagle by helicopter. They were searched, and all items on them were taken. One suspect was believed to be a high-ranking fighter because his cell phone had recordings of several speeches in support of the Taliban that he had given to various groups. The suspects were fed and housed for the night under guard and then transported to the 3rd Brigade, 205th Corps post in Shorbak the next day. The remains of the two ANA soldiers were also transported to Shorbak, sent to their families for burial.

The Afghanistan Poppy Eradication Campaign

A medevac near Nad Ali (photograph by Greg Strong).

Major Kurt Merseal

"We found out that day what we really had, and it wasn't what we wanted, but it was a place to go forward. Unfortunately, we were fragging compounds and doing what we could do to keep as many alive as we could, but at the end of the day we were hauling dead bodies in our trucks."

The Black Hawk team, ANA, and the national police set up a perimeter for the night. As always, the Black Hawk team was in the center of the security perimeter in a square with their Cougars. After they were settled and taking some downtime, the men opted to eat before going to sleep. The field rations, or MREs, included a variety of food in each different package, such as rice, mashed potatoes, corn, roast beef, spaghetti with meat, and ham and lima beans. They also featured a variety of blueberry cobbler, chipotle snack bread with cheese spread, Tootsie rolls, and Skittles. Everyone had their favorite items, but no one liked the ham and lima beans, famously known as "ham and motherfuckers."

Three • Afghanistan National Army Two KIAs

A common practice known as MRE rat fucking was taking parts of different MRE packs and leaving the rest, which frustrated Captain Settle to no end. On this day, some of the team were eating and Captain Settle was in the Cougar. He suddenly came flying out of the Cougar and yelled, "Goddamn it! When you get an MRE, you eat the whole thing. You get the whole thing! Quit rat fucking!" The team continued eating as they watched their red-faced captain. The men had a lot of respect for Settle, but right now they were laughing under their breath.

First Lieutenant Adam Cole

"That night before we were pulling security they were setting up the perimeter. The ANA would set up a perimeter, and we would get in the middle and set the Cougars in a circle. We didn't realize how cold it got when we didn't have tents. Jimmy didn't bring a sleeping bag, so when I started security I see somebody sleeping in a body bag. He slept in a body bag with holes in it on top of rocks. It was weird because when we put the ANA soldier in one it had holes in it and blood ran out all over Sandell's truck. It was weird seeing Jimmy in that bag.

"It was a shitty day. What we didn't realize is that we had ended up capturing several Taliban that day along with all their motorbikes, but we didn't have the ANA radio with us because most of the time it didn't work. Apparently the ANA executive officer had been screaming to try and get my company down there on their net; I had no idea about it. They didn't talk to any of our guys about it, and my ANA company commander just ignored him.

"When we were getting the bodies evacuated on the helicopter for the ANA, the ANA battalion executive officer had pulled his pistol and was about to kill my command commander. He had been asking for help and two of his guys were killed because they didn't move down there. Major Merseal grabbed me and said, 'Let's get the fuck out of here and just stay clear because one of us might get shot.' Shortly after that my ANA company commander was replaced, which was awesome because I ended up getting a really good ANA company commander, and my company ended up being the strongest ANA company."

The Second Day

The next morning the convoy moved back into the area north of Nad Ali to once again provide security for DynCorp while they began their poppy eradication. Shortly after the ANA and Black Hawk team set their screen line, they began to receive small arms fire and machine-gun fire. They returned fire at two different clots that the firing was coming from. As stated previously, the Taliban was very good at hiding and firing from clots, windows, doorways, and small manmade holes.

First Lieutenant Adam Cole

"The next day we were on over-watch, and there was nothing going on. I think we had a mortar round or two, and that was about it. We were hanging out and there was a couple Apache helicopters in the area. The Brits decided they were going to get some cool videos, and so they got the Apache pilots to put on a show, rolling the helicopters over and getting cool videos. There was a police mentor team made up of a lot of our scout platoon 1–30th. It was about twelve klicks [kilometers] away from us inside the canal zone.

"We were sitting there texting them on the blue force tracker back and forth, finding out how they were doing. All of a sudden, they weren't texting us back. I guess they were out dealing with an IED and it went off. It killed First Lieutenant Jared Southworth, one of his staff sergeants, and someone else. Jared was the only other lieutenant in my year group other than me that graduated from Ranger School. We were kind of asshole buddies, not good friends, but buddies. It was one of the first guys in our battalion that I knew and was killed. It was gut wrenching. We got ahold of the Brits, and they immediately directed the Apache helicopters over to their area."

The team returned fire with M-19s and .50 caliber fire. After roughly thirty minutes the firing stopped. The team subsequently kept watch for what seemed to be a couple of hours. Then a mortar round came in, and then another one. Fortunately, they weren't even close to the Black Hawk team's position.

A few hours later DynCorp completed their eradication operations and the team collapsed, and the force started moving back to FOB Eagle. During the two-day operation, DynCorp had eradicated an estimated 149.55 hectares of poppy. The Black Hawk team had five confirmed Taliban KIAs (the actual total was thought to be as high as twelve KIAs). Fourteen detainees were taken, including a high-ranking fighter.[3] The Black Hawk team had had a successful mission.

The convoy returned to FOB Eagle. At this time, the Black Hawk team got the word that the sergeant major was flying in on a helicopter to inspect the base. Major Merseal and the other staff NCOs were already occupied, so Sergeant Sowash got the job of taking the sergeant major around.

Sergeant First Class Jeffery Sowash

"The sergeant major was coming down to visit, and First Sergeant Sury and Sergeant First Class Greg Strong were gone, so I had the task of showing the sergeant major around the camp. He comes in a helicopter, and he's one of these guys and he is legit, but he is one of these guys that you just can't make smile, no way, shape, or form. He knows his stuff, and he is just hard. I am trying to do everything I can to tell him about how good morale is, how good everything is, how everything is going, and I'm walking around with him for about two hours. We had had a hard day, and he just keeps asking me questions, and I've got the right answer every time, and no smile, no good job, no nothing.

He is getting ready to leave, the helicopter is coming back in, and we are standing there, and he looks at me and says, 'Where are you going to the bathroom?' 'Well, Sergeant Major, we go out there,' pointing away from the FOB to the point away from the camp. 'We walk out into the desert a little ways, dig a cat hole and we go there.' It was still cold at the time, and he says, 'When it warms up that's going to draw flies. You need to get some PVC pipe about eight foot long, six inches around, bury it about five feet in the ground, fill it with gravel, and then pee in those, your pee tubes, so you don't draw flies.'

I had had it. I said, 'Well, Sergeant Major, do you want me to run down to Lowes and pick that pipe and gravel up and bring it back?' The sergeant major didn't crack a smile; he just turned, got on the helicopter, and left."

Four

It Was 75 Meters Away

> "I told Greg Strong that morning before we left that something was going to go down. I wasn't sure what; I just had the feeling. I told Greg Strong, 'Stay after it today. I have a bad feeling today,' and we boarded the Cougar."—Captain Greg Settle

February 21, 2009

The early morning air was cold as the Black Hawk team prepared for its latest mission. Some men were hitting the "Decision Maker" with diarrhea while others ate an MRE. First Lieutenant William "Snacks" Sandell, per his nickname, was stuffing his pockets with candy bars, crackers, and packs of Skittles.

Captain Greg Settle was moving about, checking on the ANA soldiers and trying to organize them, which was a challenge in and of itself. That morning, Settle didn't feel right. He had a gut feeling that trouble was brewing. He continued preparing for the mission, checking on the supplies, checking his men, checking the equipment, but the ominous feeling didn't go away.

The convoy was lined up and ready to move out. Settle told his men as they climbed into the War Pig, "Be on your toes today, guys. I have a feeling something is going to happen." The convoy now being ready, they moved out. A couple of miles down the road, someone radioed, "We need to take five." Diarrhea had hit again.

The Afghanistan National Army, the Afghanistan National Police's Poppy Eradication Force, DynCorp and the Black Hawk team had another mission—this time in an area west of Nad Ali near Checkpoint

Four • It Was 75 Meters Away

Red 18. The operation would be on the near side of the canal. The Black Hawk team would execute its tasks by establishing the outer cordon through a series of screen lines and blocking positions around three sides of the target area for eradication. The order of march was to be 2nd Advising Team (Thumper), 3rd Advising Team (Wizard), HQ Advising Team (Redman), and then 1st Advising Team (War Pig). A British contingent would also move with the force for additional support and would travel in one of the M-1151s. The advising teams would position themselves based on the scheme of maneuver that the Kandak commander had developed. The Kandak commander assigned the Kandak's executive officer, Lieutenant Colonel Wahed, as the commander for the operation. 1st Company would cover the southeastern corner of the screen as a strong point; 2nd Company would cover the remainder of the eastern position of the screen; and the 3rd Company would cover the remainder of the southern screen line.[1]

A couple of hours into the convoy movement (with some necessary five-minute breaks), the unit began to set up the screen lines. Captain Settle was out of his Cougar and giving instructions to his ANA company commander to maneuver him into position on the screen line. He heard a pop in the distance, followed by a puff of white smoke. A few seconds later, there was an explosion about a hundred yards in front of him, followed by a second strike fifty or sixty yards closer. Settle broke into a run for the back of the Cougar. As he got there, another explosion hit just under the front of the Cougar. Both front tires were blown out, and the front fenders were blasted apart. Smoke engulfed the Cougar. Sergeant First Class Greg Strong (Big Papa), located in the gun turret, hit the deck of the turret in taking cover.

Captain Greg Settle

"We established a screen line, and we had Afghans on our left and right, and I was outside the truck working with the Afghan company commander, trying to position his men, most effectively utilize his heavy weapons and employing ours as well. We started receiving mortar and machine-gun fire. Then a few RPGs came in. We found out later that that was standard ops for what the enemy would do: they would throw in some mortars, machine-gun fire, and RPGs to see what we would do. I thought, 'That is getting really close.' Then suddenly I noticed large explosions walking in real close to the front of my truck. I thought, 'Man, that is coming in quick and fast,' and started running toward the back of the truck. All I remember is suddenly the front of the truck was just engulfed. The explosion blew out both front tires. Then machine-gun fire began hitting all around me and down both sides of the truck. I could see it hitting the ground between me and the truck and all around the area. I read a book on a guy in combat that said things begin to go into slow motion as they are happening, but I didn't believe it till that day. It's amazing what the body does when it gets put in positions like that. It was pretty intense, and I admit I was really scared. Then I heard one of the guys on the radio scream, 'Settle is down. Settle's down,' 'cause I mean it was just watching it from outside. I got on the radio and said, 'I'm down, guys,' 'cause smoke was everywhere, and I looked down and patted my legs to see if I had any, I was looking for blood and holes, there wasn't any."

Sergeant First Class Greg Strong

"It was one of our first major ticks, and I was in the turret. I saw something out of the corner of my eye. It was an AGU-17, which is like our Mark-19, and it fires three different grenades each time it fires. I got on the radio to Settle and said, 'What is that?' because I could see it walking in on us. About the time I said that, Settle noticed it and ran behind the Cougar. The grenade hit right in front of the truck. It blew both front tires out, and the fenders on the Cougar were thin and the rest armor, and the explosion put holes in the fenders. I thought, 'It got him,' I really did, and I stopped firing and got on the radio. I'm like 'Settle, are you all right?' No answer. I'm like 'Settle, you okay? Settle, you okay?' and he says, 'Wait a minute, I am still checking,' because he had shrapnel go between his legs and he didn't know if he was hit or not."

Captain Settle ran to the side of the Cougar and jumped in as both screen lines began receiving heavy small arms, machine-gun, recoilless rifle, RPG and mortar rounds from the southeast. Several RPG rounds went off close to Captain Settle's team (which included First Lieutenant Brian Mays, Sergeant First Class Greg Strong, Private First Class Zachery

Four • It Was 75 Meters Away

Tyminski, and Mustafa Noori, the team interpreter) and the 3rd Advising Team (First Lieutenant William Sandell, Sergeant First Class Jeffery Sowash, Staff Sergeant James Ressel, Private First Class Michael Garcia, and interpreter Mahammad Noor).[2]

The ANA and the Black Hawk team returned a rain of fire with small arms, .50 calibers, and M-19s. The fight continued for about one hour, and then the firing from the Taliban stopped. The screen was then relocated to the north as the eradication operation continued. Concerned about subsequent resistance from the Taliban, Major Nick Johnson exited 2nd Advising Team's vehicle (Thumper) and relocated his position to the Joint Forward CP (Joint CP), located approximately 150–200 meters away and approximately 50 meters from Redman's location. At the Joint CP, Major Johnson began to work with the Kandak's executive officer to conduct the operation and transfer messages from the Kandak and DynCorp to Major Merseal and the advising teams. Then, if needed, Major Johnson would relocate to Redman's position to assist the mortar crew because he had experience as a mortar platoon leader.

A few minutes after the units had relocated their screen lines, they began to receive direct fire and indirect fire from mortars from the southeast in the vicinity of the southern screen line. The Black Hawk team initially thought the firing was from an AGS-17, but they soon realized it was from anti-aircraft gun ZSU-23.

The ANA commander decided to maneuver their influence on the operation. They took a vehicle, with one or two additional officers, forward of the Joint CP to reconnoiter two clots that were to the immediate front. One clot was closer to the Joint CP and one closer to where the 2nd Advising Team was positioned. The small arms fire coming from the clot near the Joint CP and HQ Advising Team was mostly suppressed.

The vehicle returned from its reconnoitering mission, but as the team arrived at the Joint CP, mortar and 107 rockets were fired, with rockets exploding immediately behind the ANA 1st Company and its advising team, near the Joint CP, and in the eradication area. One rocket hit approximately twenty to thirty meters behind the position in which Lieutenant Colonel Wahed and Major Johnson were operating with the Joint CP and landed approximately fifty meters further to the rear.

The Afghanistan Poppy Eradication Campaign

Two rockets that hit near the Joint CP and within the eradication area did not detonate, and Major Johnson called the DynCorp EOD team in to do an assessment and controlled detonation. EOD identified two UXOs (one HE and one WP). Major Johnson relocated the Joint CP, and the DynCorp EOD team detonated both of the rockets.

In the meantime, the advising teams and the ANA soldiers were hammering the clots with M-19s, .50 calibers, and small arms fire. The attempt to suppress the Taliban was somewhat effective, but it was difficult to penetrate the thick walls of the clots. Major Merseal decided to call in air support.

Staff Sergeant Kyle Campbell

"I remember Captain Settle on the radio telling what happened, and I was again gunning in Major Merseal's Cougar. I was in the gun with a Mark 19. I locked on that T and E, and I just raked the whole area from side to side. While I am doing that, I can remember me and Sergeant Rabbitt were the only ones on the team that had any past experience with mortars. I was on a mortar crew when I was in Iraq, and then Sergeant Rabbitt was a mortar man. We had an ANA mortar team with us, and Sergeant Rabbitt jumped out of the vehicle to closely monitor the ANA team because they weren't quite as proficient as we were. I am taking the building from side to side with the Mark 19, and then the other trucks came up and got on line. The Taliban was returning fire with recoilless rifles and whatever else they had. Sergeant Rabbitt screamed at me all at once, saying he heard a DSHK firing. DSHK is like the Russian equivalent to our .50 caliber; it's a very heavy caliber, and he swears it was one of them and rounds just missed him and scared him to death. He yells, 'Shoot that fucking building, shoot that fucking building!' I had been shooting at it the whole time. I'm shooting and he is dealing with the ANA and they are stumbling all over themselves trying to get the gun set up. The ANA mortars were the most lethal and devastating weapon we had available to bring to the fight. Anything else, we got to call for help, whether it's artillery or attack helicopters or close air support.

"I put a few more boxes on Mark 19 on the building. Major Merseal asked if Sergeant Rabbitt was okay and if the mortar gun was set up,

Four • It Was 75 Meters Away

and I tell the major I should go help him. The major said go ahead, and I jumped out and ran over to the mortar site. Me and Sergeant Rabbitt took over the guns, started working the mortars, and the ANA handed us the ammo. We fired the mortars for a while, and the ANA lieutenant said we needed to move our position because the Taliban knew where our position was by now. We grabbed everything, and it seemed like we ran forever. We just started running, and there was rounds and explosions going off all around us. We finally get to a spot where the ANA lieutenant said was okay and started setting up again. I was glad the ANA lieutenant was starting to take control. It was something that happened a lot.

"We set up the gun, and Sergeant Rabbitt setting the sites and I am taking the assistant gunner role. I shifted the bipod, and he got the sites finally set, and we fired a round and it was right on that building. We were excited; we had the ANA to set the fuses, and we just started dumping mortars on the building. I'm the only one with radio to the JTAC that's in the helicopter, and the helicopters are sweeping back and forth, and I heard the JTAC talking to a fighter pilot. He got cast on station and was going to start dropping bombs. I didn't have another radio that I could contact the team with, and it was a dangerous situation. I hear the countdown, so I run back to the truck, I open the door and I scream at Major Merseal what I know, and then I run back to the mortar tube to keep dropping mortar rounds onto the building. Then I get more information and run back to the truck and open the door and scream what I know at Merseal. It was a lot of running.

"I remember on one trip back to the truck Major Merseal had worked his way from the TCC, where he is just kind of sitting with a computer in front of him, and he has worked his way up to the turret. He's got all the radio mics stretched out in there and hung up in different places. He's got his clipboard, he's like trying to take notes and shoot the Mark 19 at the same time. He is like just multitasking way beyond his capability, but he is trying to get it done. He yells at me and says my Mark 19 is fucked up, like it's my fault, right, that it isn't firing right. I get in there, and it was simple user error. When you put the belt in and you close the tray, there is a little like two teeth that slide back and forth, and they have to be in one position, not the other, when

The Afghanistan Poppy Eradication Campaign

you close it. If it's in the wrong position, it won't feed the belt, so I popped the tray and slid the teeth over and told him, 'You have to have this in like this.' I closed the tray, and he was shooting and happy again. That was a really long day. That might have been the most ordnance from close air support we had dropped in a day.

"It started out with the French aircraft and JTAC were calling for 500- and 1,000-pound bombs right off the bat for these buildings. The French have their own rules of engagement, and they start with the smallest, least possible collateral damage and work up, but they were starting with the large bombs because the machine-gun fire coming from the buildings and rocket fire was very intense. I had raked that same building over and over with the M-19 but found out later that it is hard to shoot through a clot because the walls are so thick nothing but a rocket will go through them. Even our .50 calibers wouldn't penetrate them. About the time the 1,000-pound bomb hit one end of the building, we saw about four or five Taliban run like hell out the other end and into another building. I aimed in on it with the M-19, and some of the ANA soldiers were near that building and waving their arms like crazy so I would know where their position was and not hit them. About the time the Taliban entered the second building, a 1,000-pounder hit that building, and that was the end of that fight. It was beautiful. I mean, you couldn't get better timing than that."

Major Kurt Merseal

"I have never put my initials on anything as big as the 1,000-pounder we dropped. We had anti-aircraft gun, an AGS-17, the Mark 19 version blasting at us, and I'm in the turret, and I'm trying to be the team commander, but I'm the only guy in the truck. I'm hammering on the Mark 19, trying to think who's with me, but Kyle Campbell was out running the mortar crew for the Afghans, and they're dropping mortars, and all the other company mentors are out doing the same thing with their troops, and the fire fight was raging pretty good.

"I got a 1,000-pounder lined up for us and told them which compound I wanted to disappear. We were close at this point, and pressure incapacitation range on something that heavy is significant, and we needed to be a good distance back. It was easy to get our guys down,

Four • It Was 75 Meters Away

but I knew the Afghans would be up walking around, doing whatever, and when that thing cooked off it was going to rock them and probably render them unconscious. I had given JTAC the information, and we had 30 seconds to splash. My guys were running around trying to get the Afghans down on the ground during the heat of the battle, which is a real challenge, and we were at 5 seconds to splash. When the 1,000-pounder hit the compound, all that happened was a little dust flume. You could see it go through the roof and just a little poof of dust. The 1,000-pounder was a dud, so now what do we do? JTAC said from the distance it was dropped it had to be about 50 feet in the ground. What we did then was drop several other big bombs on it. I don't think it ever went off, but the bombs left a huge crater in the ground."

The 1,000-pounder ultimately ended the fire fight with the Taliban. The two clots that all the firing had been coming from were no longer there. In short order, DynCorp completed the eradication operation after covering 100 hectares. The screen lines were collapsed, and the force began to move back to FOB Eagle.

The convoy had about a two-hour trip back to FOB Eagle, but for Captain Settle and his team in the Cougar War Pig, it seemed like ten hours. When the AGS-17 had exploded in front of the Cougar, the explosion had blown both front tires out. The MRAP Cougar is designed to be drivable even with blown tires in that it has steel hubs inside the tires so that it will still be mobile. However, in this case they were traveling on the sand, and it was like trying to steer a railroad car in a sand pit. No one was more grateful to be pulling into FOB Eagle with the War Pig than Captain Settle's team when they finally arrived.

The men engaged in their usual routine when they returned, hitting the chow hall first. It was curry and rice that evening, but the cold drinks of soda and water were the best part of the meal. Then they cleaned the weapons and the Cougars of empty shell casings from the day's fighting. However, regardless of the combat situation, the poor living conditions, and the lack of good food, there was always a sense of mischief at work among the men. That included the commanding officer, Major Kurt Merseal (also known as BBK). He and First Sergeant Sury were close friends. They also liked to pull pranks on each other.

The Afghanistan Poppy Eradication Campaign

The men on the team would generally go out in the desert, dig a hole, defecate, cover it and return to the FOB, but Sergeant Sury couldn't do it; he always had to go on the "Decision Maker," their improvised "toilet." The men had taken some tarps and erected walls around the "Decision Maker" to give some privacy, but anyone who used it could still be seen from the outside.

The team often made MRE bombs, which consisted of a gallon plastic jug filled with water. Then they would take a heating element from the MRE packages, place the heating element in the water and screw the lid down. After the heating element got hot enough, it would explode, making a sound so loud people nearby would think they were receiving incoming rounds. Major Merseal had found a larger bottle than the regular gallon one and filled it with water in preparation for his joke. At this time, Sergeant Sury was on the "Decision Maker," and Merseal quietly approached the tarp, set the bottle down, loaded it with the heating element, screwed the lid on and quietly walked away.

Sergeant First Class Greg Strong

"Major Merseal and First Sergeant John Sury were really close. They were in the same truck together during our missions. They were always trying to get the best of each other with pranks, especially with MRE bombs. First Sergeant Sury couldn't go to the bathroom without the 'Decision Maker.' We had set it out from the FOB and put a little tarp around it so the guys had a little privacy, but your head stuck up above the tarp.

"Sury went to use the bathroom and was sitting on the 'Decision Maker.' Major Merseal made an MRE bomb, but he used a bigger water bottle and he wrapped the heating element in a piece of paper when he put it in the water. It was kind of a time diffuser. It floated in the paper till the paper got really wet; then the heating element sank and started heating up. I'm telling you, when that thing went off, it sounded like a 107mm explosion.

"First Sergeant Sury yelled and busted out of the tarp with his pants down and fell flat on his face. Everyone busted out laughing so hard because we didn't know what was going on, and we just heard the boom and looked up and saw Sury coming out of there with his pants

Four • It Was 75 Meters Away

down and falling flat on his face. He got up, pulling his pants up and yelling, 'I'll get you fuckers for this!' He found out that it was Major Merseal, and from then on it was on. It was a contest from then on who was going to get the best of the other."

Given that the Taliban would have been observing the FOB, they had to have been on the alert when they heard Sury yell, "I'll get you fuckers!" The first sergeant (known as "Storm" for his temper) was certainly having a storm.

The laugh over, the team began to settle down for the night. It had been a long day, and tomorrow would be another day of fighting eradication operations. As they fell asleep, their thoughts were likely of the day's events and Captain Settle's close call. They may also have thought of what tomorrow would bring. For First Sergeant Sury, however, his thoughts were probably "How am I going to get even with that fucking Merseal?"

Five

Within Inches

"I pulled my hands in and set the binoculars down, and just as I looked up a woop went by me. I mean, it was a black flash. I could feel the breeze, and I was like in my mind 'What the fuck?' but all that came out of my mouth was 'Wha?'"—Sergeant First Class Greg Strong

February 24, 2009

The Afghanistan National Army's (ANA) CNIK, in conjunction with the Afghanistan National Police's Poppy Eradication Force (ANP PEF) and DynCorp, was conducting a joint operation in Nad Ali with the area bordered by checkpoints Yellow 40 in the southwest, Yellow 41 in the southeast, Yellow 31 in the northwest, and Yellow 32 in the northeast. This operation would be the first day of conducting eradication operations within the Governor's Food Zone.[1]

Since the operation was a transition from opening in the open desert, the Black Hawk CNIK would execute its mission by establishing over-watch positions on the near and far sides of the crossing point, checkpoint Blue 2, and then the outer cordon through a series of screen lines and blocking positions around the four sides of target area 19 for eradication.

The ANP PEF would establish a series of pickets to secure the route, since there was only one route in and out of the area. The northern screen line was the road from checkpoints Yellow 31 to Yellow 32; the eastern screen line was the road from checkpoints Yellow 32 to Yellow 41; the southern screen line was the road from checkpoint Yellow

Five • Within Inches

40 to Yellow 41; and the western screen line was the road from checkpoint Yellow 31 to Yellow 40.

Major Kurt Merseal intended to make a tactical move from FOB Eagle to the assigned eradication area. The order of march was the 1st Advising Team (War Pig), 2nd Advising Team (Thumper), HQ Advising Team (Redman), and then the 3rd Advising Team (Wizard). A British contingent (JTAC), as usual, would accompany the force in one of the MRAP Cougars. They would move behind Redman and position themselves near that vehicle to provide communications to close air support (CAS) assets.

The advising teams were to position themselves based on the scheme of maneuver developed by the Kandak Commander. He ordered the 1st Company (ANA) to cover the western and southern screen lines, while the 2nd Company (ANA) had two platoons located on the near side of the crossing point (Blue 2) and two platoons on the far side to ensure that this point was open to the force. 3rd Company (ANA) was ordered to cover the northern and eastern screen lines. The Black Hawk CNIK was to establish a strong point at checkpoint Yellow 31 to deny the enemy access to the area from the northwest. The team would deploy a dismounted force (Captain Greg Settle, Captain Quincy Springs, First Lieutenant Adam Cole, First Lieutenant William Sandell, Staff Sergeant James Ressel, Specialist Kegan Anderson, and an interpreter, all under the command of Captain Settle) to block any enemy attack.[2]

The members of the convoy had begun to move into position when they were suddenly hit by a haboob. The word *haboob* comes from the Arabic word *habb*, meaning wind. A haboob is a wall of dust resulting from a microburst or downburst. The air forced downward is also pushed forward by the front of a thunderstorm cell, dragging dust and debris with it as it travels across the terrain. In short, it is a sandstorm.

In Afghanistan, sandstorms can reach heights of ten to fifty feet. These storms also have wind speeds of at least twenty-five miles per hour, so they can blow up quickly (within a matter of minutes), as happened to the convoy on this day. The soldiers soon found themselves caught in the middle of blowing sand and wind with zero visibility.

The Afghanistan Poppy Eradication Campaign

Sandstorm on the way to mission; mission cancelled because of sandstorm (photograph by Greg Strong).

Sergeant First Class Jeffery Sowash

"We went out to set up a screen line and a sandstorm came through. We were only in the screen line for less than an hour when it hit. The sand was blowing sideways and really hurt when it hit you. We couldn't see fifty feet in front of us, and that was really dangerous because the Taliban could come in close on us to fire on us. I mean, they could have come up to within fifty feet of us before we saw them. We had to get everybody out of there and back to the FOB without basically being able to see. We really didn't have radio contact with the Afghan soldiers that were with us, mainly because their radios didn't work half the time. We were going around rounding them up and letting them know we were not going to stay and that we were going to go back to the FOB.

Five • Within Inches

"We finally rounded everyone up and set out for the FOB. We used flares so the vehicles behind us could see us and we didn't lose anyone. It took a couple of hours slow moving, and we finally got back to the FOB. It was a relief to get in the tents and out of the sand. Being in the gun turret and getting hit in the face with sand coming at you hurt like hell. We all got back without losing anyone or making contact with the Taliban."

The Black Hawk team moved about in the midst of the storm, making sure all the ANA troops were in their trucks as they collapsed the screen lines and prepared to move back to FOB Eagle. Flares helped the convoy stay together on the return journey. The wind gusts were well over 30 miles an hour, with sand blowing against the trucks sideways. Big Papa (Sergeant First Class Greg Strong), always positioned as the gunner for the War Pig in the turret, said it best: "That damn sand hurts like hell."

After taking an additional two hours to return to FOB Eagle (moving much slower than usual because of the reduced visibility), the Black Hawks enjoyed the chance to be out of the wind and the sand, back in the new Alaskan tents that DynCorp had provided for them. These tents were much better than the old ones, with no holes in them or leaks from the rain. In addition, showers had been built, along with porta potties. Life was still not good, but at least it was better than before.

The next morning, the convoy returned to Nad Ali, following the same plan from the day before. Once all the screen lines were in place, DynCorp began the eradication process. About ten minutes into the operation, ANA PEF and DynCorp began to receive heavy small arms fire, machine-gun fire and RPG rounds at checkpoints Blue 8, 15, 16, and 17. The firing from the Taliban was ineffective in that the rounds were not hitting close to their positions.[3]

Meanwhile, Captain Settle's War Pig was set on a hill on overwatch. It was quiet. Captain Settle was on the computer, and Sergeant First Class Greg Strong (Big Papa) was in the turret, scanning back and forth at the clots roughly one hundred meters in front of them. He thought he could see movement. He put his binoculars down for a minute and then raised them and scanned again. "There is something

The Afghanistan Poppy Eradication Campaign

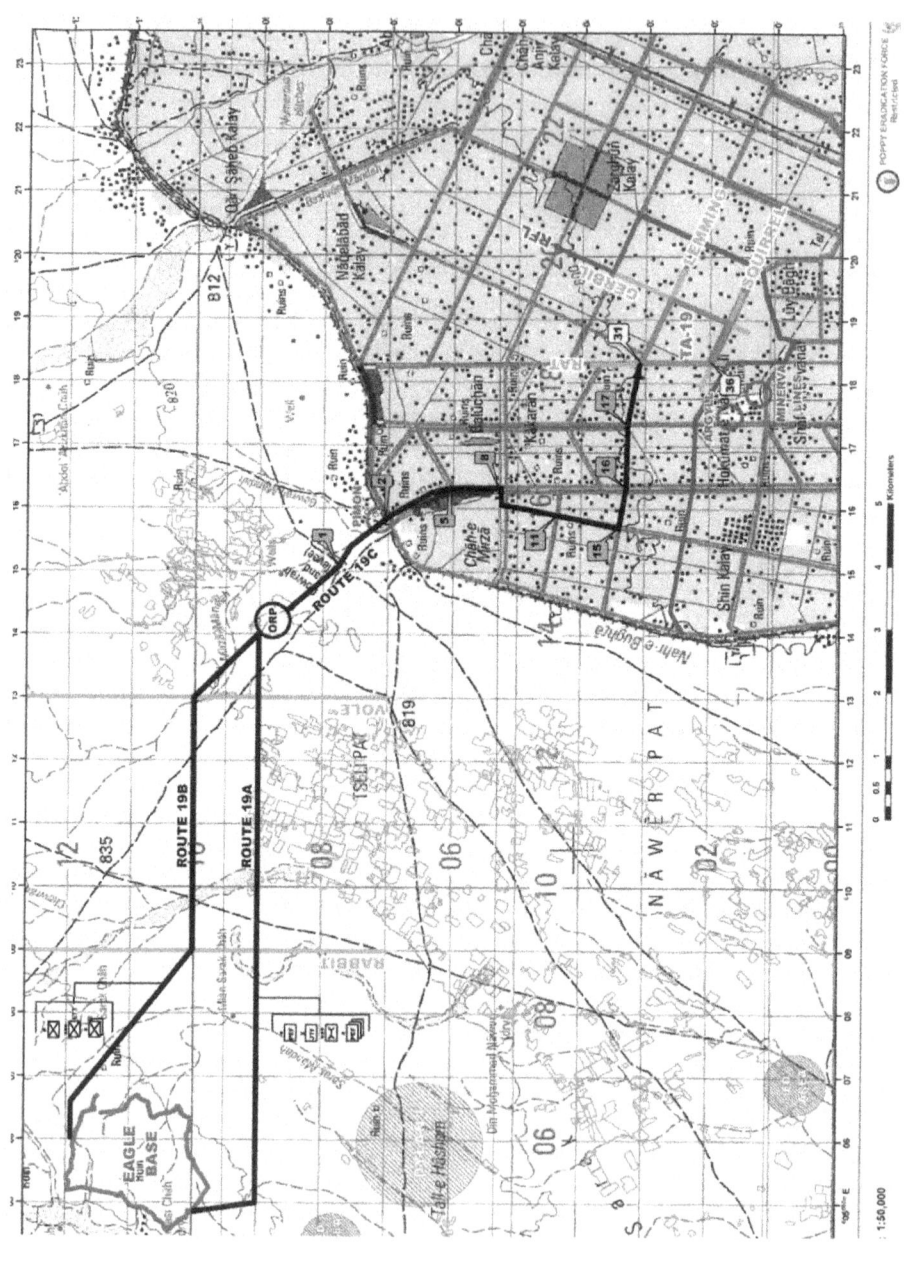

moving over there," he thought. He got on the radio and called Captain Settle with his concern. Settle told him to keep an eye out but not to overreact.

Sergeant Strong laid down his binoculars and decided to grab a bite to eat—something he rarely did in the turret. At that same time, First Lieutenant Williams had to relieve himself. He got out of the Cougar and went to the back. The back walls of the Cougars slant at an angle, so when one of the men had to go, they would go to the back, pull their pants down, squat, and lean again the angled wall of the vehicle. Williams had just put his back to the wall of the Cougar and Sergeant Strong had just ripped open an MRE package when a black flash passed inches by his head. Then a huge explosion struck a line of trees directly behind the Cougar.

Sergeant First Class Greg Strong

"We were on this hill near Nad Ali, and we were across from a canal had had over-watch. There was this little clot about a hundred yards from us, and I kept telling Captain Settle, 'There is movement over there.' He says, 'No, there's not.' I kept telling him, 'I am watching people move around over there, and they are kind of suspicious.' Captain Settle goes, 'Come on, man.' He always tells it like it is and said, 'Look, man, as close as we are, they don't want to die any more than we do.' I'm like 'You got a point,' so I finally calmed down and decided to take a break.

"I opened up an MRE, and sure enough I hear this dun, dun, dun. I thought it was a Mark 19, so I decided to take the binoculars, and I'm looking over the turret. I got my arms resting on the turret and I am panning. I see the Mark 19 and no one fired, and I heard no slash either. I didn't think anything about it, and so I pulled my hands in and set the binoculars down, and just as I look up a woop went by me. I mean, it was a black flash. I could feel the breeze, and I was like in my mind 'What the fuck?' but all that came out of my mouth was 'Wha?.' "I got 'wha?' out, and behind us was a line of trees, and it hit a tree and

Opposite: **Map of operation for February 24, 2009, near Nad Ali (map courtesy Greg Settle).**

The Afghanistan Poppy Eradication Campaign

Unexploded 107mm rocket round (photograph by Greg Strong).

exploded. The tree wasn't solid enough for it to completely fragment, and that's how I got the piece back that was still in the tree. I'll tell you, I was really scared for one, and shook up to boot. Finally, Captain Settle had to tell me to shut the fuck up on the radio. I was talking like a stupid man.

"That area was probably the scariest because we went there three times and there was one way in and one way out. It is right by a canal, and that thing was about sixty feet wide and Lord knows how deep. Water just runs rapid through it, and what they were trying to do, because the roadway was right next to it, was to plant IEDs so that we would have to stay on the roadway and they could disable the trucks. They wanted the IEDs to flip the trucks over into the canal because they knew that if we got in the water in the trucks, we couldn't open the doors. The doors are just dead weight because they weigh about six hundred pounds apiece; plus, the current being heavy, you're not going open any doors—you're just going to drown.

"The first time we went in, it was pretty much unscathed. We went in, fought like hell, and came out. The second time we found a couple IEDs going in and nothing on the way out. The third time there was enough IEDs that we really weren't effective eradicating the poppy. We went in and did our mission, but there wasn't a whole lot of eradication because it took us so long to get in, about a half a day.

"The funny thing about the rocket was I hardly ever ate in the turret. I ate Slim Jims and little stuff to get me through the day, but that day I didn't have any. That's why I decided to eat an MRE that day. I had just opened it when that shell went off and everything went crazy. It's amazing what you get used to. You know the old expression, it's amazing what you can get used to in this line of work. You know, like, we named all of our trucks, and I didn't know why the fuck Captain Settle came up with the name War Pig, which was the name of our truck. I have a real mechanical background and can make anything run, and our truck never left us, and the truck was hit the most while we were there, from mortars to machine-gun fire to rockets. Like one time we had a mortar round go off right by us and shook the truck so damn bad it shook all the dust off of it. Major Merseal was like 'You guys okay?' He heard the boom and saw all the dust and thought we had got a direct hit. Captain Settle said that's why he named it War Pig."

Captain Greg Settle

"We were pretty much in the same location and established a good screen line, and the bad guys fired a 107mm rocket right in front of my truck and missed my gunner's head. He said it was within three inches, and I said, 'Well, you would be dead if it came that close,' but it was really close and scary. I never soiled my pants, but I could have that day. It came really close and exploded right behind the truck. Greg [Strong] was always calm, cool, and collected. He made things happen, but that day, when that happened, he was rattled. I said, 'Greg, calm down.' He says, 'All right, I am calmed down.' I said okay, but he never calmed down much that day. It was just another day in Afghanistan and another life lesson."

The Afghanistan Poppy Eradication Campaign

First Lieutenant Jason Williams

"We're on an intersection. We had poured into the area, so Brian Mays, Greg Strong, Greg Settle are at our position in the south. We hadn't made any contact that day going in, so a pretty quiet day. I had to poop, and so the V-shaped hall, that's kind of how you poop out there: you lean up against the hall and then poop. So, anyway, it's under the truck, so no big deal. I'm sitting there on the back of the truck, eating an MRE, and Brian had got out and walked to the other truck and was on the other side talking to the gunner. Next thing I know, I hear something scream by, and it's this extremely loud, deafening explosion in the trees. They had shot a rocket, and it just missed Greg Strong's head. It hit the tree and there was branches and shit going everywhere, and then they just opened up on us.

"We started returning fire, and it took me a minute to figure out what just happened. Brian is coming, running back, and they pulled the truck up a little bit, and here is this pile of shit that I made now at the back of the truck. There are rounds hitting everywhere, and Brian is running toward the truck and just almost stops when he gets to the pile. He jumped in the truck, and I grabbed him and pulled him the rest of the way in the truck.

"Someone got on the radio and said they had an Afghan soldier down. He had been hit in the neck, and it had went down and was lodged in his lung because he was lying down when he got hit, so they needed another guy over there. I run over there, and they start working on him, and I asked the doc what he needed. He says, 'I need tape,' and so I'm like 'all right,' so I get in this bag, and we all had our medical bags arranged the same, and so I grab the bag, and his bag was a mess. He had shit all over his bag, so I had started throwing stuff and looking for the tape. And this wounded kid says, 'Sir, calm down.' I say, 'I'm calm if you're calm; your bag's a mess,' and I damn near wanted to break the kid's jaw right there.

"Anyway, we get this guy out of there, and it's an irrigation canal, and I am thinking it is one or two feet deep, so I stepped right into it, like right in the middle of it. It was pretty wide, and it was about four or five feet deep. I drop the guy and go in the water, and we are still taking on fire, and he starts floating down the canal because the water was moving pretty good, and so we finally get the guy out of there. I ran back to the truck and told Captain Settle that he needed to get the Afghans to stop shooting mortars because the helicopters won't come in until they quit shooting mortars. I get an interpreter, can't remember which one, and we went on a one-hundred-yard dash, and getting shot at, there's rounds snap, crackle, and pop, and we finally get there and get them to stop. Then the fire died down a little bit, and the helicopters came in and got the wounded Afghan soldier."

First Lieutenant Adam Cole

"We get to this little intersection, and there's a row of trees on one side and a row of buildings on the other side, and we figured at some point we were going to take fire from it. There were also buildings to the south. We put my truck at the intersection, Settle takes his truck and pushes a little bit south of me, and then the ANA walked in and set up. I finally get back in the truck, and I'm like 'I can finally relax. I can take it easy a little bit,' and I popped my Kevlar off.

"Since we were just sitting there, it kind of got the adrenaline out of my system. All of a sudden, there's a boom right in front of me, and it is in one of those little trees at the northwest part of the intersection. At first, I thought it was an IED that I had missed somehow, and I was like 'You got to fucking be kidding me,' I had checked everything. But it was a 107mm rocket that had been fired from a house at Settle's truck, and it just missed Greg Strong and almost hit him in the head. He said he felt the damn thing go by him, and the Taliban opened up with small arms fire at the same time.

"I'm looking at my ANA, or actually Settle's ANA. My ANA were with a new company commander able to operate a little more independently, and they're all up and moving, except one guy, who actually had his body armor on, but he was kind of rolled over on one side and he'd been sleeping because they took naps any time they could do it. I could see just a little bit of red on his body armor, and I was 'Aww, shit, doc, let's go.'

"We got out of the truck, and I don't know how I got out of my truck because I was right next to one of those shit ditches that are

The Afghanistan Poppy Eradication Campaign

everywhere that are like four feet deep, and somehow I got out of the truck. We are running, rounds hitting everywhere, and we get over there, and the guy had got hit in the shoulder and it had gone straight in and tumbled into his lung. He had already lost a lot of blood. The doc gets over there a little later, and I told the doc to start working on him.

"I started popping off rounds because we were taking fire from the buildings off to our east and it was kicking up all around us. RPGs were hitting all around us, and the doc was only 19 years old and his hands were shaking, and I was like 'Doc, don't worry, everything is good.' About that time a couple rounds hit right in front of us. He was like 'What was that?' I said, 'They are just bad shots.' I was just trying to get him to calm down.

"I'm trying to think how I am going to get this guy back across the ditch and decided we were going to need some help. I got on the radio and called Settle and told him I needed some help to get this guy moved. He sends Willy, and Willy is like a big dumb animal—God bless the guy, I love him to death—but he comes running over and ready to help. He's like 'Doc, what do you need?' The doc says, 'I need some tape.' He was trying to stuff the wound as much as he could because it was internal. The doc said, 'We got to get him out of here or he is done.' I was still having fun firing at windows and doors because I didn't have anything else to do. Willy just rips that bag open, and, in his words, he was just looking for the tape and didn't know where it was, but to us it looked like he just ripped the bag open and was throwing things. The doc, 19-year-old E-4, said, 'Sir, calm the fuck down.' Willy yells back, 'If you're calm, I am calm!' I was laughing in my head because in the middle of a fucking fire fight a 19-year-old specialist just told a lieutenant to calm down.

"Willy and I are dragging this guy back across this little shit ditch, and when you don't have equipment on you could jump across, but when you're carrying a body that's pretty much dead weight, and we get to the ditch, and Willy slips and drops the guy right in the shit ditch. I jump in to get him, and I just remember thinking I had torn out the crotch on my pants and there was no protection—my balls were now exposed to Afghan sewage.

Five • Within Inches

"We hauled the guy back in, got him out, and then about that time Settle had called in British artillery on the wrong house, and there was some confusion translating the call for fire. Then the Apache helicopters got on station and lit up a couple other houses, and that ended the incoming fire."

The fire fight had broken out in all the areas of the screen lines. The Wizard (with First Lieutenant William Sandell, Sergeant First Class Jeffery Sowash, Staff Sergeant James Ressel, Private First Class Michael Garcia, and Zabullah the interpreter) and Redman (with Major Kurt Merseal, Captain Mark Foth, Sergeant First Class Sean Rabbitt, Staff Sergeant Kyle Campbell, Major Robert Bailey and Nirab the interpreter) provided additional suppressing fire along with the War Pig.

Captain Greg Settle

"We were down in Nad Ali, which is a network of canals and dirt roads, and the Afghans like to flood the areas to grow their poppy, and we were there doing our eradication mission. We were providing security for the ANA army while they provided security to the Afghan police, who was actually doing the eradication, but again it was our truck with Greg Strong and Lieutenant Mays, and I think Lieutenant Adam Cole was there with us and maybe one other truck. Everybody was sitting up on the hill. Anytime we went down in the area we would always take a couple of companies, and everyone else would stay on the hill and provide over-watch up top.

"We started taking a beating, and I knew we had some British 105 artillery support not more than a couple klicks from our location, so, being a former artillery, I decided to call in artillery support on the bad guys. I got ahold of JTAC, and I said, 'We are getting hit really bad.' I said, 'Here is our location,' and gave them my grids and told them where the bad guys were and gave them their grids. I said, 'Can you run me a fire mission?' and they confirmed they could. He drops a couple rounds. I told them I had a visual on the rounds and made adjustments, and every time I made an adjustment the rounds went exactly the opposite direction. This went on for a while, and then we went for a fire for effect.

"Afterward, we were still getting hit pretty good. I called and said, 'You were pretty close on the fire for effect. Man, let that stuff go,' and

The Afghanistan Poppy Eradication Campaign

I got on the radio and told all the guys down because the artillery was going to be dangerously close and heavy; button up, because it's coming in.

"It is one of those experiences I will never forget. When the dust settled from the artillery coming in, we may have suppressed the Taliban a little bit. But they were still hitting us pretty heavy from a couple of locations. By that time we had called in a couple of Apache helicopter gunships. They suppressed the Taliban in a short time."

With the eradication operation completed, the screen lines were collapsed and the units moved into a new area for the night. As they settled in to get some sleep, Sergeant First Class Greg Strong stared at the hunk of shrapnel he had in his hand. It was from the rocket round that had just missed his head earlier in the day. Big Papa, as his men called him, knew just how close he had come to death. He would carry this hunk of shrapnel with him wherever he went in the future as a reminder of how lucky he was to be alive.

The Next Day

The following day, the ANA, ANP PEF, Black Hawk Advising Team, and DynCorp once more set screen lines near Nad Ali, and DynCorp renewed eradication operations. The Black Hawk team had been expecting a big fight, but nothing was happening.

Sergeant First Class Greg Strong

"The next day we went out again, and we were set up, and I told Freddy Falmier to keep an eye out; I was going to take a quick minute and eat. As soon as I opened the MRE, shit went south—here comes the fire fight. So then the third day we went out, and we were really expecting to draw some fire. We were hyped up for a really big fire fight, but nothing happened. Pretty soon Sergeant Brewer came on the radio and said, 'Hey, Strong, you open that MRE yet?'"

Prayer time must have ended for the Taliban, which is usually when they would start their fighting, because all hell suddenly broke loose. Small arms fire, machine-gun fire, RPGs, and now mortars were dropping in. The ANA opened up with suppressing fire, and the Black Hawk team broke out the .50 calibers, M-19s, M-203, and AT4. The enemy fire was coming from clots about a hundred meters from their left front. The fight got so intense that Captain Settle called the British for artillery support. Shortly thereafter, the firing from the Taliban slowed, and then after about an hour the firing stopped completely.

The eradication operations were concluded, and the screen line began to be collapsed. Captain Settle and Captain Springs from War Pig, First Lieutenant Sandell from Wizard, Major Merseal from Redman, and First Lieutenant Cole from Thumper then dismounted from their vehicles and began to ground guide the vehicles through the narrow canal roads.

While the convoy was traversing the canal, the Taliban renewed its assault of small arms, machine-gun, and RPG fire. DynCorp also reported that they were receiving fire from the east. The ANA CNIK force began to move faster in order to engage the enemy. It created a gap in the line, and the Taliban dismounted the vehicles to suppress the enemy fire. Finally, once all the vehicles were through the canal, the firing stopped.

The convoy made its way across the desert and back to FOB Eagle. The men were totally worn out from the two-day mission. Much to their relief, as they got out of the vehicles, the smell of cooking food filled the air. As they hurried to the chow tent, they found that grilled lamb chops had been prepared. They filled their trays and dug in. As usual, the lamb chops had very little meat and were extremely tough; the only good thing about the chops was that one had to chew a long time before the meat could be swallowed, so they lasted longer. On the plus side, they also had tater tots—American food. Life was good.

Six

AT4 Round Misses Compound

"I was like 'wooo hooo,' and I'm high fiving, and all I remember seeing that AT4 go right over the top of a building I was shooting at. Who knows where it went, but it didn't go where I wanted."— Major Kurt Merseal

February 28, 2009

Fight, eat, and sleep—this had long since become routine for the Black Hawk team. However, some concerns had been raised about whether the MRAP Cougars were the best vehicle choice for their mission.

First Lieutenant Adam Cole

"We had a discussion with Major Merseal about using Humvees instead of the MRAP Cougars when we were going into these canal areas because they were smaller and easier to maneuver. And we wouldn't have to ground guide going through the narrow canal roads. Major Merseal refused to do it. The Humvee isn't built to take an IED blast, which would put the advisor teams in danger. It was a great decision, because there were guys who died because they were riding in Humvees. They are a lot more maneuverable and make a lot tighter turn, but they don't take an IED blast worth a shit. Merseal said, 'I had rather lose one of you by small arms fire ground guiding than to lose an entire truck of people in a Humvee in an IED blast.'"

Six • *AT4 Round Misses Compound*

The decision having been made, the Black Hawk team loaded the Cougars with supplies and ammunition in preparation for another mission in Nad Ali. This would be the second eradication operation conducted in the Governor's Food Zone; ANA CNIK, ANP PEF, and DynCorp would now be working within the area bordered by checkpoints Blue 8 in the southwest, Blue 9 in the southeast, Blue 5 in the northwest, and Blue 6 in the northeast.

As before, the Black Hawk team would provide security by establishing an over-watch position on the near side of the crossing point (checkpoint Blue 2), and then the outer cordon, through a series of screen lines and blocking positions around the four sides of target area 21 for eradication. The northern screen line would be the road from checkpoints Blue 5 to Blue 6, and the southern screen line would be the road from checkpoints Blue 5 to Blue 8. The Black Hawk team was

Convoy on the way to operation in Nad Ali (photograph by Greg Strong).

The Afghanistan Poppy Eradication Campaign

to take the convoy to the area tactically with the 1st Advising Team (War Pig), 2nd Advising Team (Thumper), HQ Advising Team (Redman), and 3rd Advisor Team (Wizard), followed by the British contingent (JTAC) in the MRAP Cougar named Pogue Mahone.

The Kandak Operations Officer had assigned the 1st Company ANA to cover the northern screen line. The 2nd Company ANA would cover the southwestern screen line. However, the soldiers would not place themselves on the road, in order to mitigate the likelihood of being in contact with the enemy. The 3rd Company would cover the southern screen line, while the Black Hawk team was to establish a strong point on the western screen line.[1]

The convoy moved out across the desert, making its way toward the targeted area for eradication. There was no enemy contact on the way, but there were the usual calls about having to "take five." A

Afghan truck hits IED near Nad Ali (photograph by Greg Strong).

Six • AT4 Round Misses Compound

couple of hours later the units reached the crossing point at checkpoint Blue 2.

As the units moved into position between checkpoint Blue 2 and checkpoint Blue 5, the Taliban opened up with direct small arms fire and indirect mortar and RPG fire from a position in the northeast. The firing was ineffective at the time, but a few rounds did land five to fifteen meters from the vehicles. The ANA troops and the Black Hawk advising teams began to fire on a series of clots where the shooting was coming from, and then they started receiving fire at checkpoint Blue 15. The firing continued for about an hour, and then it stopped—and so had Sergeant First Class Greg Strong.

Sergeant First Class Greg Strong

"We took our 100-round .50 caliber cans and a Mark 19 can on a mission. We were in a fire fight, and I am laying lead down range, and I ran out of ammo. We are in a hell of a fire fight, shit is pinging all over the place, so I reached down and grabbed an ammo can, opened it, loaded it in the 50, and sat down. Captain Settle couldn't hear the 50 firing, so he radioed and asked if the 50 was down. I said like no, but he wouldn't let me answer because he just kept asking if the 50 was down. 'Strong, is the 50 down?' I'm like no, and he says, 'Strong, is the 50 down?' I am trying to answer, but he has his hand on the radio button. I can't get the answer to him, so I'm trying to yell through the turret. Finally he let go of the button, and I said, 'The 50 is not down, I am down; it is just too damn hot for me to stick my head up. When shit calms down, I will stick my head back up.' Everyone was listening to the radio and thought it was funny as hell."

As the force continued to move ahead with the eradication operation, the Taliban opened fire again. This time the assault was coming from the northeast inside the eradication area. The firing was AK-47 and PKM fire only—no mortars or RPGs. The Black Hawk team and ANA returned fire, and the fighting only lasted about fifteen minutes.

For the rest of the operation it was quiet. When the task was complete, DynCorp had eradicated 12.6 hectares. The screen lines were collapsed as the force prepared to withdraw. The withdrawal was covered by Redman (carrying Major Kurt Merseal, Staff Sergeant Kyle

The Afghanistan Poppy Eradication Campaign

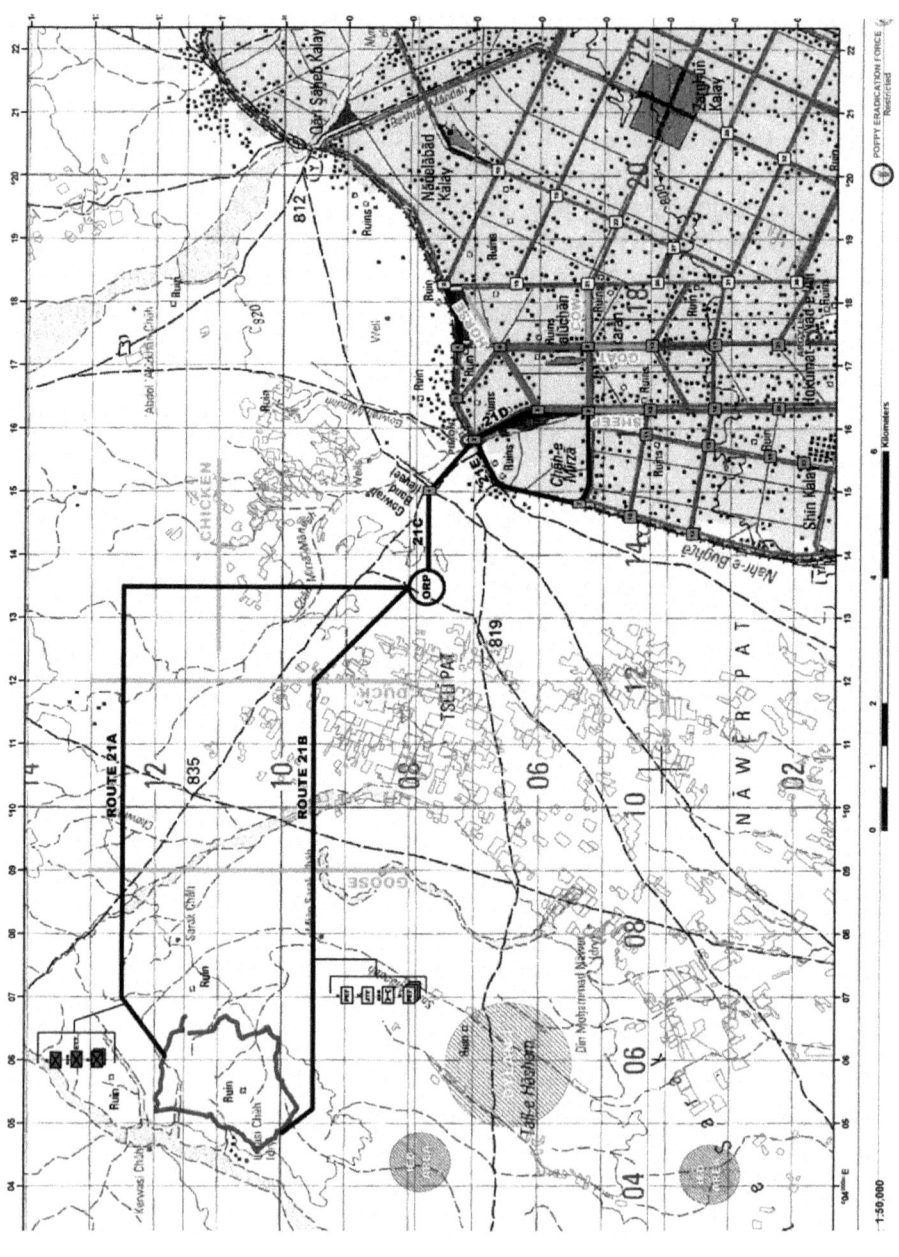

Six • AT4 Round Misses Compound

Campbell, First Sergeant John Sury, Captain Mark Foth, Major Robert Bailey, and interpreter Mirab) and Wizard (First Lieutenant Troy Kemper, First Lieutenant William Sandell, Staff Sergeant James Ressel, Private First Class Michael Garcia, and interpreter Zabullah Safi).

As the withdrawal got under way, the Taliban opened up again. This time the fire was coming from the southern screen line and the northeast—still inside the eradication area. The firing was direct small arms fire and indirect mortar fire.

First Lieutenant Adam Cole

"No shit, there we were again, did a dismount when we were leaving after a mission, and we are getting hit, and we get out and start ground guiding to make sure a wheel doesn't drop right off into one of those ditches. I'm sitting there, and Merseal is grabbing an AT4 to shoot at this house. I'm like 'Oh, this is going to be awesome, the boss man's going to light up this house with an AT4 and just destroy that wall.' He is all excited, and he fired that thing, and it has to be in orbit now. I mean, he shot that thing so damn high. We started using them after that, and John Sury fell in love with them and started shooting them at everything after that."

Major Kurt Merseal

"We'd gone inside the canal zone in a town called Nad Ali, and no doubt not a friendly place, and very few people went in there and operated. We took a huge force in there, and the road networks were real restricted. You always had a canal on one side, if not both sides, and the roads were not designed for trucks like ours. One of the biggest fears I had was turning a truck over. We had experienced it, turning a truck over, becoming fixed; then you're there for however long, and they can hit you from whatever direction they want to. So what we would do is when we would come into these intersections, we'd get out of the truck and one person would ground guide these trucks through these narrow intersections, and some of them it would take literally

Opposite: Map of operation for February 28, 2009, near Nad Ali (map courtesy Greg Settle).

The Afghanistan Poppy Eradication Campaign

MRAP Cougar on over-watch near Nad Ali (photograph by Greg Strong).

minutes to get a truck past them. You'd have to back up, pull it forward, jock it around, and try to get through the intersections without dropping a wheel off and turning the thing over in the canal.

"We'd been a little spat most of the day, been in contact, and we were frustrated with DynCorp because of where they had us going that day. That day was just insane, but we figured we could do it relatively safely. We did it and we provided security all day, cleared a route and had contact at the same time, but on the way out DynCorp was in a position to lead us out; otherwise we were going to have to try to pass them, which was next to impossible because of the narrow roads. They started out normally, and we had always cleared a route for them, but they were leading, and they started getting hammered with small arms fire and RPGs. I'll never forget. I mean, you could hear them on the radio, and they were pretty hyped up. It was RPG after RPG, just one after another, and I was watching and thought, 'Good grief, how many RPGs can these guys have?' They weren't hitting anything.

Six • AT4 Round Misses Compound

"We'd give it a little time, give it a pause because there was nothing we could for them, but I thought, 'Before we roll in there I am going to give them enough time that they will probably be out of RPGs.' It came our turn, and I had Troy Kemper driving, Campbell was gunning, and then I had an MD that was assigned as our medic. You know, there are not many teams that get a full-fledged doctor, but somehow we got one. He's riding in the back, and we pull up where the good stuff had been happening. They were shooting at us, but wasn't hitting us, and Campbell is rocking on the M-19. Then he switches over to the 240, and I'm getting pissed off because all I can see is brass and all these links falling in the truck. I yelled at Campbell and said, 'Do you really have to shoot that much? Do you know how long it is going to take us to clean this truck?'

"We pull up a little bit, and we are like the second truck, and we are getting ready to go through the intersection, and I'm watching the guy and can't remember who it was—could have been Settle ground guiding through this tight ass intersection on these dirt roads—and I can see the bullets kicking up around him, and I'm like 'Son of gun, I am going to die ground guiding the truck and not really the way I want to go out.'

"We have an AT4 in the truck, and so I was like 'You know what, before I get shot ground guiding, I'm shooting a freaking AT4,' so I jumped out, and it had been a long time since I had actually had my hands on an AT4. It's an anti-tank weapon. I get out, man, I'm like 'All right, I remember how to do this,' and I get it all armed and I got my target. I know where they are shooting from when I come around the front of the truck, and things are just rocking and rolling. Things are just going on everywhere, you know, and it's coming in and it's going out, and I'm looking over there, and Settle is ground guiding, giving the drivers signals, and he has dust kicking up all around him.

"Boy, I come around the truck, and I hit the trigger on that son of gun, and I kind of jerked. It was a dud, and I step back by the truck and I'm like 'Damn, what do I do now? I've got this live missile that just misfired, and I'll be damned if I am going to leave it here for the truck,' and I don't even think I aimed, and I kicked that baby off, and it went off, and somebody actually videoed it and it was a huge explosion.

"I had disappeared in the smoke and they thought I was gone, but

The Afghanistan Poppy Eradication Campaign

I was like 'wooo hooo,' and I'm high fiving, and all I remember seeing that AT4 go right over the top of a building I was shooting at. Who knows where it went, but it didn't go where I wanted, but that was the beginning of shooting the AT4s. We shot a lot of them after that day. My claim to fame is I shot the AT4, and, long story short, they give me a lot of shit over missing the compound. They said, 'How do you miss a compound? It was a house. How do you miss a freaking house that is four hundred yards away?' I just said, 'Well, after the misfire I don't know what happened.' I was a little nervous, but anyhow I lost it right over the top of that house, but I swear there were some other compounds and I swear I hit one of them. Anyway, I moved up the truck, got out, and ground guided my truck through. We got everyone out, and no one got hurt that day."

The force made it through the canal with anyone getting wounded or killed and continued to a predetermined destination to set up security for the night. The men were inside their perimeter, and Captain Settle went to get an MRE. However, he was less than pleased with what he discovered.

According to Greg Strong: "Captain Settle was on a rage. I mean, he is pissed again. It isn't the first time. The guys are MRE rat fucking again. Everybody wants something good to eat, and the guys would go through the MREs and get the best stuff and leave the rest. You go in to get an MRE, and half of it is missing. Captain Settle went to get an MRE. He came out yelling, 'God fucking damn it! When you get an MRE, you eat it. Quit rat fucking!'"

The men weren't sure if the Taliban had heard Captain Settle's "Quit rat fucking!" order, but the men of DynCorp must have. They surprised the Black Hawk team with a gift of steaks. The Black Hawks were certainly surprised, but with DynCorp there always seemed to be a problem of some kind, and this pattern held true with the steaks. DynCorp had brought steaks, charcoal, and lighter fluid, but they forgot to bring anything to cook the food on. In the desert, that is a problem.

Sergeant First Class Greg Strong

"At night we would put the Cougars in a square inside the ANA perimeter. Some of the guys would sleep on the ground, some took

Six • *AT4 Round Misses Compound*

cots, and I slept in the back of the truck. My vest was in the turret, so that all I had to do was stand back to the turret and I was ready to go. We had some great instances out there. Merseal and John Sury are great outdoorsmen. DynCorp thought they would be smart and bring us steaks. They brought steaks and charcoal, but no grill to cook them on. We all went and found the biggest flat rocks we could find, and we washed the rocks. We started the charcoal and put the rocks on top of them and then cooked the steaks on the flat rocks. Then the DynCorp people said, 'Hey, can we have one?' We responded, 'Hey, dudes, you left us out in the cold and we dealt with it. You deal with it.'

"That night we had to pull fire watch, but it's kind of hard to pull fire watch if you don't have a fire. Merseal goes, 'We will build a woodless fire.' We all had this crazy look on our faces. He dug a cat hole about two foot by two foot and about two foot deep. Then he poured JP8 diesel fuel in it. Then he put on a layer of sand and poured it again. He did that over and over until he was at the top of the hole.

"He lit the fuel, which was slow burning. As that layer of fuel began to die down, you could remove the layer of sand and the next layer of fuel would burn. We had a fire all night. It was the coolest thing I ever saw."

Seven

The IEDs

"Bill Brewer was my driver that day, and he is screaming at Willy, 'You dumb son of a bitch,' and it popped, and Willy was like 'Oh, fuck!'"—First Lieutenant Adam Cole

March 3, 2009

The men of the Black Hawk team were up and busy preparing for another mission. They were going back into the Canal Zone, with its flooded canals and narrow roads. This would be another joint operation with ANA CNIK, ANP PEF, and DynCorp in Nad Ali. For this mission, they would be working on the canal road within the area bordered by checkpoints Blue 14 in the southeast, Blue 15 in the southwest, Blue 10 in the northwest, and Blue 11 in the northeast. Many of the fields had been flooded previously to prevent the impending eradication.

The Black Hawk CNIK would establish the outer cordon through a series of screen lines and blocking positions around three sides of the target area (22B) for eradication. The northern screen line would be the road from checkpoints Blue 10 to Blue 11; the eastern screen line would be the road from checkpoints Blue 11 to Blue 15; the southern screen line would be the road from checkpoints Blue 14 to Blue 15; and the Western screen line would be the canal road, covered by the Afghanistan National Police from checkpoints Blue 10 to Blue 14.

In order for the convoy to move safely to the eradication area, three MRAP Cougars (Redman, Pogue Mahone, and Wizard) pushed out while the Afghanistan National Army's M-1115 Humvee and three

Seven • The IEDs

IED crater in road near Nad Ali (photograph by Greg Strong).

or four ANA Rangers moved to the high ground west of canal to monitor the area and establish the over-watch position. The order of march in the convoy was HQ Advising Team (Redman), M-1151 Humvee, HHC Advising Team (Pogue Mahone), and then the 3rd Advising Team (Wizard). HQ Advising Team (Redman) covered checkpoint Blue 10, Pogue Mahone checkpoint Blue 14, and Wizard checkpoint Blue 18.

Approximately thirty minutes after the first group departed, the second group, consisting of the reconnaissance force, left the FOB. The order of march for this force was 2nd Advising Team (Thumper) followed by the 1st Advising Team (War Pig). The second group also brought the Afghanistan National Army Kandak to the position. The advising teams positioned themselves based on the scheme of maneuver that the Kandak Commander developed.

The Kandak Commander assigned the intelligence officer as the commander for this operation. The intelligence officer ordered the 1st Company to cover the southern portion of the screen, while 2nd Company

The Afghanistan Poppy Eradication Campaign

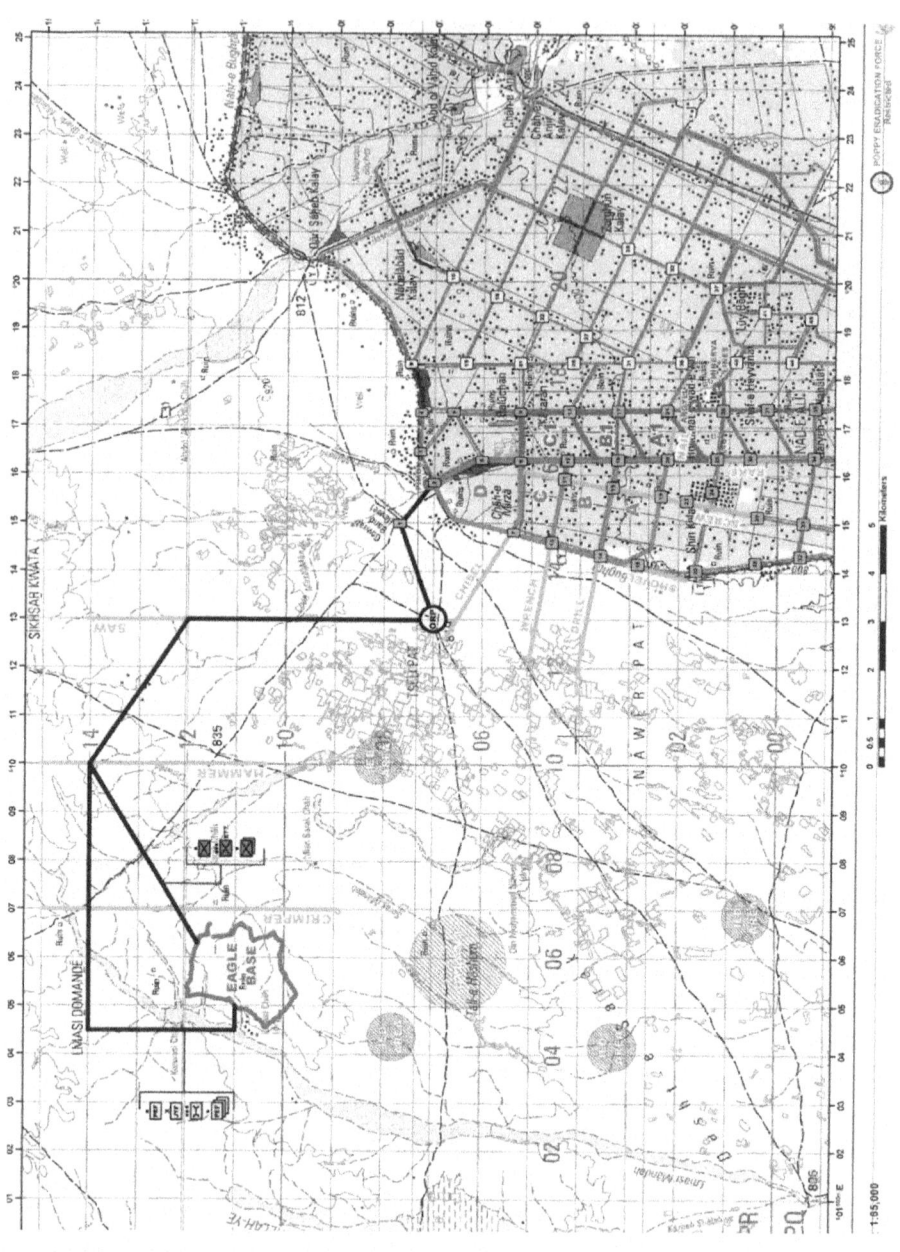

Seven • The IEDs

covered the northern portion and 3rd Company the eastern portion. The Black Hawk Team CNIK positioned their remaining MRAP Cougars near checkpoint Blue 15 in order to hold the southeastern corner. That position had been a strong point during previous operations, receiving indirect small arms fire and indirect mortar fire from a structure overlooking the area. From the strong-point position, those in Thumper and War Pig (Captain Greg Settle, First Lieutenant Adam Cole, First Lieutenant Brian Mays, First Lieutenant Jason Williams, Sergeant First Class Greg Strong, Staff Sergeant Freddy Falmier, Staff Sergeant William Brewer, Specialist Kegan Anderson and interpreters Haroom Ahmed and Mustafa Noori) could dismount and assist the Afghanistan National Army.[1]

The Black Hawk team successfully crossed the canal road entrance at checkpoint Blue 2 and began to clear the route. Although the ANA clearing team had moved ahead of the force to clear the route, the Black Hawk team decided to clear the western screen line again. This was the second time that the Black Hawk team had utilized this route, and there was only one way in and one way out, so it was critical to secure the road..

The 2nd Advising Team's interpreter, Haroom Ahmed, alerted the Black Hawk team that he had obtained a metallic signature with his metal detector. The team verified the signature and contacted the DynCorp EOD. The EOD soon arrived on the scene and conducted a controlled detonation approximately 300 meters south of checkpoint Blue 10. Approximately fifty meters ahead of the previous spot, another metallic signature was obtained by Haroom Ahmed, and it, too, was verified as an IED and destroyed by controlled detonation. The clearing continued, putting the operation behind schedule. As a result, the DynCorp program manager, Kirk Sessin, moved forward from his position to the clearing position to find out what was holding them up. Major Merseal ordered the clearing team to continue to make sure the road was cleared and safe. Merseal also repositioned Redman from its position in the high ground overlooking checkpoint 10 to ensure that the

Opposite: **Map of operation for March 3, 2009, near Nad Ali (map courtesy Greg Settle).**

clearing team was not interfered with or rushed. Captain Settle contacted Major Merseal by radio and informed him that he had taken care of the situation with Kirk Sessin; Redman then returned to its over-watch position.

First Lieutenant Adam Cole

"We had just gone down in Nad Ali inside the canal zone some narrow roads, and it was kind of a shit show because again DynCorp decided they wanted to go down the same exact route to an area right next to where we had just been. Major Merseal had messed up his back really bad, and so he was going to sit in the over-watch on the other side of the canal zone, and me and Settle were taking our companies in. Since it was the second day we had gone in there, we decided we better check the road for IEDs. Our biggest worry was that they were going to have an IED big enough to drop a truck in the canal, and then we would lose an entire vehicle crew. We were in MRAP Cougars, and those things can take an IED blast and be fine. They weren't like the RG-13s that I've seen—two or three of them get ripped in half and the whole crew get killed.

"Settle, Willy, and my interpreter Bob were out checking the road for IEDs, and we weren't looking thoroughly because we thought, 'Well, they probably haven't gotten a chance to put much in.' We had Bob carrying the metal detector, and we would have him to check a spot here and there, and we were getting close up to this intersection. I said, 'Check there, Bob,' and nothing, so I told him another spot and nothing. All of a sudden, he's like 'Sir, I think I find something.' I was like 'What the fuck did you find, Bob? Give me that thing.' I grabbed the detector and go over and get a beep. I said, 'That could be anything,' and in the army they always tell you use a non-metallic probe so you don't create a connection and set it off.

"I pull out my handy pocket knife because I'm smart again, and I slide it down in the dirt. It looked packed on top. What they do is sprinkle water to get it to harden a little bit, but underneath it was real loose. The knife slide right down, and I pulled up a black wire. I was just like 'fuck,' and this was a couple of weeks after Southworth had died pulling up an IED, and I am just sitting there, everything going through my head,

Seven • The IEDs

Poppy field near Nad Ali (photograph by Greg Strong).

like 'If this thing goes off, I'm not even going to have time to think anything. I'm just going to be gone and hamburger,' and so I just hold my hand up and stop the truck because it was moving right behind me.

"Settle and Willy had already walked on beyond this, and they were up by the intersection, and I just make a big circle around the dirt, and I walk back to the truck really calmly because if it was command wire, I didn't want them to know I found it and set it off. I was like 'Hey, can you get on the radio and have DynCorp get their EOD guys up here?' Willy—I love that guy, he is one of my best friends—but that dumb son of a bitch walked back up there because he didn't believe that I had found an IED, and he walks right down to it and sees the wire and goes, 'Oh, shit!' and then walks back calmly to the truck.

"We called them [the EOD team] the Kiwi and the Ging because one of them had red hair, and it was a big joke because I was the other

The Afghanistan Poppy Eradication Campaign

IED crater near Nad Ali (photograph by Greg Strong).

ginger and he was the other ginger, and the other one was from New Zealand. It was Kiwi and Ging, and they were really good guys, really solid. I said, 'I just marked it out there if you guys want to pop it and see what happens.' They just took a little block of C4, went out, and dropped it and popped it, and the next thing you know we had a waist-deep crater that's both-arms-width wide, and I was like 'Holy shit!'

"Bill Brewer was my driver that day, and he is screaming at Willy, 'You dumb son of a bitch!' and then it popped, and Willy was like 'Oh, fuck!' I was like 'All right, we better start checking the shit a little bit closer,' so I go up to the intersection that Settle had just been at and I go by the crater, and maybe not another one hundred meters at the side of the turn at the intersection, and I tell Bob to check that and there's another wire. I pull this one, and it's a little clear wire; you could see the copper wiring on the inside, and it had clear insulation on it. I stopped the truck again and go through the whole same shit show with

Seven • The IEDs

Kiwi and Ging. They're looking at it and said they thought this one may have a command det on it, and we had these jamming devices on our trucks and you could see when it was actively jamming it. It had this little yellow light that would start flashing. I asked Bill if it was flashing, and he said, 'It was flashing a lot when you were out there—almost solid.'

"About that time we had this lieutenant colonel come down wearing his baseball hat, and he won't talk to us because Merseal had just finished chewing his ass. I hated that guy. He goes up to Kiwi and Ging, and I am close enough I can hear him, and he says, 'Why are we moving so slow?' He just wanted to get on the road, and they told him they had two IEDs they were checking out. He asked if they were sure they were IEDs, and there was a crater in the middle of the first one, and they said they were checking it out. He said, 'Maybe they are old IEDs,' and I am thinking, 'Wat the fuck does that matter?' and about that time Merseal is on the radio because he is watching from over-watch. He tells Settle, 'You want me to come down there? I will kick his ass.' He was really getting worked up. Settle calls him back and says, 'You can't do nothing, boss; your back is fucked up right now.' We checked the rest of the road. We pulled extra metal detectors and checked every bit of the road, but we didn't find any more IEDs. We moved at a snail's pace while we checked it out and finally got into position."

The Black Hawk team was in position, and the eradication operation was under way. Suddenly the Black Hawks began receiving heavy direct small arms, machine-gun, and effective RPG fire and indirect mortar fire from the Taliban in the vicinity of checkpoint Blue 15. An ANA soldier was hit, and First Lieutenant Cole and Specialist Anderson began to treat him while First Lieutenant Mays coordinated with the ANA to ground evacuate the wounded soldier to the Casualty Collection Point (CCP) located at checkpoint Blue 14. Unfortunately, the soldier died; the inbound medevac helicopter would return to its station until conditions were appropriate to land and retrieve the body for transport to Shorbak.

A 107mm rocket hit about 15 meters from Captain Settle's War Pig and about 5 meters from Thumper. The rocket was immediately followed by a heavy volume of small arms fire and RPGs. Staff Sergeant

The Afghanistan Poppy Eradication Campaign

Falmier and Sergeant First Class Strong immediately began suppressing a compound where the 107mm round was fired from with .50 caliber machine guns from Thumper and War Pig, respectively.

The ANA CNIK also began to fire on the compound with RPGs and small arms fire. As the ANA force was fixed in its position due to having sustained a casualty, Captain Settle contacted Opal 63 element (British JTAC) for close air support (CAS). First Lieutenant Williams then coordinated with the ANA to readjust their front lines to reduce the likelihood of a friendly fire incident.

Wizard (carrying First Lieutenant William Sandell, First Lieutenant Troy Kemper, Staff Sergeant James Ressel, Private First Class Michael Garcia, and interpreter Zabullah Safi) and Pogue Mahone (Major Johnson, Captain Mark Roth, Staff Sergeant William Thorpe and the interpreter Shurab) opened up with suppressing fire on the structure. Staff Sergeant Ressel also attempted to provide support with his Barret sniper rifle. The structure being out of range, the suppression stopped because the fire was ineffective.

First Lieutenant Adam Cole

"Everybody got to experience sitting in a truck all day with Freddy Falmier. He was sitting there pulling security, and he was in the truck by himself. We had pulled our truck back and Merseal was in overwatch, and Freddy is sitting there by himself and he gets bored. When Freddy gets bored, he likes to shoot warning shots. Since he didn't have anybody to talk to in the truck, he just keyed it over the net. We're just sitting there, and I'm just looking at Settle and said, 'I deal with this every day.'

"Freddy's like 'I see a guy moving, I'm going to fire a warning shot.' Then we hear a 50-round burst on the .50 caliber, and everybody is like 'Oh, God.' Then Freddy goes, 'Well, he's down.' Then he says, 'I'm going to lob a 203 round over there and see if I can get them to move.' He does it and then says, 'Nope, he ain't moving.' And it is like 'Oh, God, he is just calling this whole thing in on net.'

"For some reason we decided it was a smart idea to carry a squad automatic weapon. We get up to this little ditch, and I'm loaded down with an AT4 rocket, machine gun, and a shit load of rounds and body

Seven • The IEDs

armor. That ditch wasn't wide. It wasn't any big deal—you could probably step across if you stretched a little—so I jumped and barely make it, and then everybody after me is like tossing their shit across and we just tore through houses.

"The third special forces group operated out of that area, and they had apparently taken out a command cell the night before and it was quiet. I made a joke that the guy who kept shooting at us all day had just one piece of brass, and he was just going back to reload it because it would be one shot and then be a couple minutes, and then we would get another pop shot. It was nice and quiet most of the day until they pulled out the anti-aircraft gun. We pulled in a Marine pilot to blow it up, but he couldn't find it.

"They didn't hit us really bad until we started moving out, and then they lit us up with everything they had. We didn't end up getting the anti-aircraft gun. I think a couple weeks later 3rd Special Forces ended up getting it."

The force was advised from Opal 63 that an AH 63 and AH 64 were on station for support. Captain Settle's dismounted team and Redman coordinated with Opal 63 and Widow 33 (another British JTAC) initially for artillery fire, but they were unsuccessful, as the bracketing of the rounds could not get to the target. The target compound was then marked with .50 caliber rounds for the attack helicopters on station to reduce collateral damage. The AH 64 fired two hellfire missiles and 30mm rounds and obtained direct hits. The structure was completely destroyed.

The eradication operation concluded with 7.9 hectares of poppy destroyed, and the screen lines were collapsed. The force then began to move back to FOB Eagle. On this day there was no fire from the Taliban as the force left the area.[2]

After returning to the FOB, it was time to eat and take showers—and for First Sergeant John Sury, it was time for payback. He had two gallon plastic jugs filled with water and was waiting for Major Merseal to visit the porta potty. Once Merseal was inside, Sury waited few minutes and then walked quietly behind the porta potty and placed one jug on each side. He unscrewed the lids, dropped the heating elements in the jugs, screwed the lids back down, and then quickly walked away.

The Afghanistan Poppy Eradication Campaign

A short time later, BOOM, BOOM! Had there been an NFL scout standing nearby when Major Merseal exited the porta potty, he would have been on the team of his choice, because he hit that door harder than any NFL lineman in the history of football. The door flew open, and he came out running while pulling his pants up at the same time. First Sergeant Sury was bent over with laughter, and the other men burst out laughing too. Major Kurt Merseal, known as "By the Book" (BBK), had just gotten his comeuppance.

Eight

Smoke Signals

"I mean, it's amazing what you figure out, but what you don't know and how primitive it is—you're like 'Is that really what they are doing? Are they really sending smoke signals?'"—Sergeant First Class Greg Strong

March 11, 2009

The next operation would take place over a five-day period from March 8 through March 12, 2009. The Black Hawk team would perform its part of the mission on March 11, 2009. This was yet another joint operation with the ANA CNIK, ANP PEF, and DynCorp in an assigned eradication area northeast of Nad Ali near Highway 1. The Black Hawks would establish a series of screen lines and blocking positions around three sides of the target areas for eradication. The eastern screen line would be the 20 grid line; the southern screen line, the 20 grid line; and the western screen line, the 26 grid line. For the mission, Major Merseal conducted a tactical move from the patrol base to the assigned eradication with the 1st Advising Team (War Pig), 2nd Advising Team (Thumper), HQ Advising Team (Redman), HHC Advising Team (Pogue Mahone), and 3rd Advising Team (Wizard).[1]

The Black Hawks took their positions based on the plan created by the Kandak executive officer, Lieutenant Colonel Wahed. He had assigned the 1st Company to cover the western screen line, the 2nd Company to cover the eastern screen line, and the 3rd Company to cover the southern screen line. The northern screen line (Highway 1) would be covered by the ANP PEF. The Black Hawks would establish

The Afghanistan Poppy Eradication Campaign

a strong point in the southwestern corner of the screen area because the commander figured that if there were contact with the Taliban, it would most likely come from that area.

After all the forces were in position, DynCorp began the eradication operation. Things were quiet for a while. Sergeant First Class Greg Strong scanned the area with his binoculars, keeping on the alert for trouble.

Sergeant First Class Greg Strong

"It is funny what you learn after you had been there for a while. We knew every day we were going to fight; it was just a matter of when. The only time we knew we wouldn't fight is right around lunch time because they have prayer time, but, boy, after prayer time they would start up. It's amazing how primitive they are because we didn't realize when we first got down there, we would come up on a village and we'd be in our over-watch. We would see white smoke come out of different chimneys, and we were, like, we didn't put two and two together. We got ICOM scanners for the radio talk between the different Taliban guys, their interpreter, and they'd put green grass on the fire if they had a good firing position. If they had a good fighting position, they would make white smoke in those, which we didn't realize till later.

"I mean, it's amazing what you figure out, but what you don't know and how primitive it is—you're like 'Is that really what they are doing? Are they really sending smoke signals?' But for sure when you would see the women and children leaving the village, you knew the fight was about to start. They would kidnap the husbands and keep them there, so once we got into a fire fight, if any of them were killed, they could say we were killing civilians. They would always try to put us in a bad light that way."

Quiet time was suddenly over! Redman, Wizard, and Pogue Mahone began receiving direct fire at the strong-point position. It was direct PKM and RPG fire and indirect mortar fire coming from a structure in the southwest. Several mortar impacts landed twenty to thirty meters from Redman (carrying Major Kurt Merseal, First Sergeant John Sury, First Lieutenant Troy Kemper and the interpreter Mirab) and Wizard (First Lieutenant William Sandell, Staff Sergeant James Ressel,

Eight • Smoke Signals

Staff Sergeant William Thorpe, Private First Class Michael Garcia, and the interpreter Mahammad Noor).

The advising teams returned suppressing fire with .50 calibers, M-19, AT4, M-240B, 52mm mortars to the Taliban. Staff Sergeant Ressel also began using his Barret sniper rifle to fire at Taliban targets. Those in War Pig—Captain Greg Settle, First Lieutenant Brian Mays, Sergeant First Class Greg Strong, and the interpreter—destroyed the structure and the firing stopped. It had lasted for about twenty minutes.

During their time in Afghanistan up to this point, the Black Hawk team had learned a lot about the Taliban. They seemed primitive, living in clots that appeared almost biblical and sending smoke signals, but they could fight, and no matter how much the Black Hawks or the Afghanistan National Army threw at them, they returned day after day, trying at least to hold their ground. The Taliban also had other tactics that were anything but primitive.

FOB Eagle had been chosen because its location was beyond the reach of Taliban fire. However, that didn't account for a pick-up truck that might drive close by the camp with a mortar tube in the truck bed in order to drop a couple of rounds into the FOB. It also didn't account for the firing of mortars without setting the fuse. Many mortars were fired at the FOB in this fashion; most missed, but a few made it into the FOB, landing in the sand without exploding. The sand in many areas, including the FOB, was very hard packed, so when the mortars were fired and hit, the impact would scatter the clots of sand in all directions, much like shrapnel, and could injure or kill someone close by. In addition, if a round landed in the FOB, the Black Hawk team would have to contact DynCorp's EOD team to disarm the shell. This tied up the Kandak units, which took time away from other missions or tasks such as eradication operations.

Once DynCorp had completed the eradication operation on March 11, the screen lines were collapsed. The force then moved back to FOB Eagle. Shortly after their return, the familiar swirling sound was in the air. One round missed, and another landed in the middle of the FOB. Naturally, the DynCorp EOD team was called in. No one was injured, and after the shell had been disarmed, the men went back to

The Afghanistan Poppy Eradication Campaign

eating dinner and cleaning trucks. It was just another day in combat in the desert.

March 18, 2009

The next joint operation with the ANA CNIKANP PEF, and Dyn-Corp saw them returning to Nad Ali, this time working near the canal road within the area boarded by checkpoints Blue 2 in the north, Blue 5, Blue 8 in the southeast, and Blue 7 in the southwest. It would be the fifth time they conducted eradication operations within the city.

The prior eradication operations conducted in Nad Ali were carried out with significant enemy contact (AK-47, PKM, RPG, mortar, ZSU-23, and 107mm rockets) and only one KIA (ANA CNIK). On this occasion, the CNIK would execute its mission by establishing a series

Bags of poppy seeds captured by CNIK (photograph by Greg Strong).

of screen lines and blocking positions around two sides of the target area for eradication. The eastern screen line would be the road with checkpoints Blue 2, 5, and 8; the southern screen line would be the road with checkpoints Blue 7 and 8.[2]

The CNIK ETT was to make a tactical move from the patrol base to the assigned eradication area. The convoy was ordered to move at different times into the area so as to break the pattern of departure and to establish the screen at a time when the enemy was less likely to be prepared. The group would include the 1st Advising Team (War Pig), 2nd Advising Team (Thumper), HQ Advising Team (Redman), and 3rd Advising Team (Wizard). As was customary, the JTAC British contingent moved with the force for additional support, traveling behind Redman.

Once again, the advising teams followed the Kandak Commander's scheme of maneuver. The 1st Company covered the southern portion of the eastern screen line, the 2nd Company covered the northern portion of the eastern screen line, and the 3rd Company covered the southern screen line. The western screen line was the canal road, covered by the ANP PEF. In the meantime, the Black Hawk team would establish a strong point in the southeastern corner of the screened area with two MRAP Cougars (War Pig and Wizard) because it was likely that enemy contact would come from that direction. The Black Hawks' other teams would position two MRAP Cougars (Redman and Thumper), as well as the JTAC vehicle, near checkpoint Blue 2 to provide over-watch and additional fire support to checkpoints Blue 3 and 5.

Once past the crossing point into Nad Ali, the Black Hawk teams began to clear the route of mines. The 1st and 2nd Companies, without their respective advising teams, would clear the eastern screen line, while the 3rd Company and its advising team cleared the western and southern screen lines.

As they moved into position, they begin to receive ineffective direct small arms, machine-gun, and RPG fire, which came from the east and south, directed toward forces at positions on the eastern screen line between checkpoints 2, 5, and 8. The attack occurred shortly after the Department of State Air Wing helicopters directly

The Afghanistan Poppy Eradication Campaign

supporting the operation were hit by incoming fire and broke away from the contact. The Taliban then turned toward the forces on the ground.

Small arms fire, machine-gun fire, and RPGs were hitting close to the Redman. Major Kurt Merseal, First Sergeant John Sury, and Captain Foth from Redman and First Lieutenant Adam Cole, Staff Sergeant William Brewer, Staff Sergeant Freddy Falmier, Specialist Jason Worker, and the interpreter Ahmad Seair from Thumper, as well as the JTAC First Lieutenant Troy Kemper (on duty as driver and to assist in calling CAS vehicles) all returned suppressing fire. First Sergeant Sury returned fire with the MK-19 and M-240B. Major Merseal, Staff Sergeant Falmier, and the team with the JTAC vehicle dismounted their vehicles to return fire.

The air assets then alerted the teams to the locations from which they were being fired upon. Redman and Wizard (with First Lieutenant William Sandell, First Lieutenant Jason Williams, Staff Sergeant James Ressel, Specialist Kegan Anderson, Private First Class Michael Garcia, and interpreter Mahammad Noor) used the M-19s in indirect fire to reach targets southeast of the screen. The JTAC observed from the air, and fixed-wing aircraft destroyed one clot where four Taliban fighters were located.

The Taliban engaged the CNIK force for most of the day, including attacking the helicopters in the area, which received several hits. It was the first time that that ANA units, which included the 1st and 2nd Companies, had moved into position without the assistance of the Black Hawk team. Fortunately, no one was wounded or killed during the operation. However, there were fourteen enemy KIAs, with two of those casualties high-ranking local Taliban commanders Khadahari and Mullah Abdullah.

Upon concluding the eradication operation and collapsing the screen lines, the Black Hawk team, ANA units, ANP PEF, and DynCorp formed into a convoy and made their way back across the desert to FOB Eagle.

NINE

The Black Hawks Find the Largest IED Factory in Afghanistan

> "I walk into this house, and there's 152mm Russian field artillery rounds just sitting there and mortars just lined up, and they've got, like, det cord and rubber cement and batteries everywhere, and I'm like 'I just found a fucking IED factory.'"—First Lieutenant Adam Cole

March 21, 2009

The Black Hawk Embedded Training Team (ETT) was loading the Cougars and preparing for a six-day mission—their longest mission to date. Rather than going back to Nad Ali, this joint operation with the ANA CNIK, ANP PEF, and DynCorp would take place in an assigned eradication area to the northwest and southeast of Gershk city near Highway 1. The force would operate from a patrol base (PB1) from March 21 through March 23, and then they would relocate to another patrol base (PB2) from March 24 through March 26. As before, the Black Hawk team, accompanied by the British JTAC contingent, would make a tactical maneuver to provide security and mentoring to the Afghans. The advising teams positioned themselves based on the scheme of maneuver developed by the Kandak operations officer, Lieutenant Colonel Ghani, who was commanding the operation.

The force moved from FOB Eagle as two discrete elements (CNIK with the EET and JTAC, and ANP with DynCorp) to separate release points before linking up at the identified patrol base. The ANP and

The Afghanistan Poppy Eradication Campaign

DynCorp element left FOB Eagle approximately three hours after the CNIK because they need to link up with their logistics element that would transport the supplies and tractors required for operation. As the ANP and DynCorp moved toward PB1, several of the tractors and pick-up trucks broke down to the point that the convoy could not move. They had to stay overnight near FOB Bastion in order to make necessary repairs. The Black Hawks were advised to occupy and secure the patrol base overnight until the ANP arrived the next morning. Then eradication operations would begin based on an assessment of their capabilities.[1]

The Black Hawks reached the release point on Highway 1 and exited the road to travel across the open desert to reach the patrol base. Approximately 300 meters off Highway 1, an MTV truck from the 1st Company struck an IED. The IED was determined to be small by DynCorp EOD, but it did break two axles and destroyed the transmission, rendering the vehicle immovable. Luckily, no one was injured.

In response to the ICOM chatter of a pending attack, the 2nd Company, with its advising team in Thumper (First Lieutenant Adam Cole, Staff Sergeant William Brewer, Staff Sergeant Freddy Falmier, Specialist Jason Worker, and interpreter Ahmad Seair), held their position approximately 500 meters to the north. The HQ Advising Team in Redman (First Sergeant John Sury, First Lieutenant Troy Kemper, First Lieutenant Jason Williams, and interpreter Mustafa Noori) moved forward to provide command and control, as well as additional fire support. No contact was made with the enemy, so 1st Company ANA and the 1st and HHC advising teams in War Pig (Captain Greg Settle, First Lieutenant Brian Mays, Sergeant First Class Greg Strong, and interpreter Ramin Barack Darokhan) and Pogue Mahone (Captain Mark Foth, Staff Sergeant William Thorpe, Specialist Kegan Anderson, and interpreter Shurab), along with the JTAC vehicle (with Staff Sergeant Kyle Campbell driving) and a DynCorp EOD Team, remained with the MTV truck for security while the Kandak and the remaining advising teams moved forward to establish the patrol base.[2]

The 1st Company ANA remaining at the MTV truck determined that the vehicle was unrecoverable and decided that they would leave a platoon behind while the rest of the company, the advising team,

Nine • The Black Hawks Find the Largest IED Factory

Pogue Mahone Cougar hits IED (photograph by Greg Strong).

JTAC, and EOD moved to the patrol base. Pogue Mahone took the lead, but it struck an IED less than a kilometer from the patrol base and began to receive small arms fire from a series of clots approximately two hundred meters away. No injuries were sustained by the IED, but the front right wheel of the MRAP was destroyed.

Redman, Thumper, and Wizard (First Lieutenant William Sandell, Sergeant First Class Sean Rabbitt, Staff Sergeant James Ressel, and interpreter Zabullah Safi) left an ANA force in place to secure the patrol base and moved to the site of the blast. Local security was established, and an ANA dismounted force advanced on the clots where the small arms fire was coming from. As the ANA advanced, the exchange of fire became more intense as the ANA and the Taliban exchanged heavy volumes of machine-gun fire, RPGs, and small arms fire.

The Afghanistan Poppy Eradication Campaign

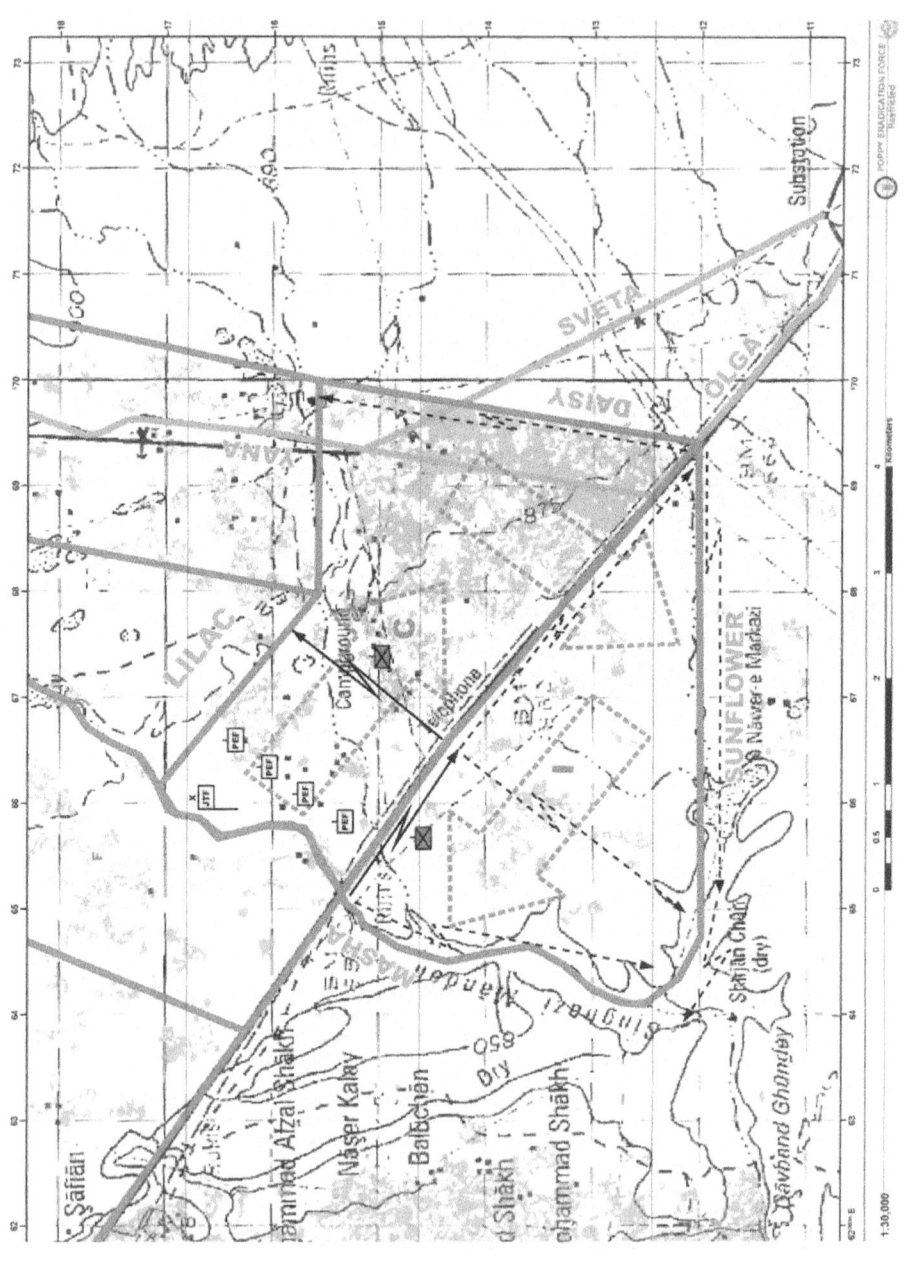

Nine • The Black Hawks Find the Largest IED Factory

After about twenty minutes, the ANA pulled back because the enemy within the clots was too strong. All the forces returned to Pogue Mahone's location to provide perimeter security, since the equipment available was unable to move the vehicle. War Pig and Thumper then returned to the ANA MTV truck. The force was receiving enemy small arms fire, and since the ANA had determined that the MTV was unrecoverable, they decided to destroy the truck. The force then returned to Pogue Mahone's location and established that area as a patrol base. The rear detachment, Major Nick Johnson and Captain Quincy Springs ARSIC-South, and Combined Joint Task Force Phoenix VIII were contacted by radio to coordinate for the recovery and repair of Pogue Mahone.

Meanwhile, First Lieutenant Jason Williams slammed his ankle in the door of the War Pig Cougar.

First Lieutenant Jason Williams

"I remember when we went to Garesh I was about to go on leave. There was just something about going to Garesh that didn't sit well with me. I thought somebody was going to die going in there. I don't know why, but I just had that feeling. I wasn't in my normal truck, and it was hit by an IED on the edge of a field, and it was like real soft sand and it was hard to move around, and it blew the tire off the whole axle, so we were fixed in place. I believe it was the Dutch recovery team, but it took like two days for them to get to us. That night it was twenty-four-hour guard on the truck. I was on the truck, and me and Troy Kemper were taking turns on the gun. He had to piss, and so we were sitting on a hill, and I got out of the truck. The doors weigh six hundred pounds, and I had stepped out with one foot and reached back in to get my gun. I thought the door had went all the way open, but it swung back and landed square on my ankle.

"The medics looked at it and immediately told me that I had a broken ankle. Some birds were coming in, and Captain Settle told me I had to catch a bird and get my ankle looked at. I was reluctant, but Captain Settle ordered me to go, so I caught a bird. When I got back

Opposite: **Map of operation for March 22, 2009 (map courtesy Greg Settle).**

The Afghanistan Poppy Eradication Campaign

Pogue Mahone Cougar hits IED (photograph by Greg Strong).

to the FOB up north, there was a bunch of Marines in the area. They had got all shot up. I just hobbled away and went on leave. I never did get my ankle looked at."

Meanwhile, DynCorp and CNIK ETT leadership were attending planned meeting and route reconnaissance for future missions in the Kapisa area. That included the CNIK ETT team chief, Major Kurt Merseal, who would attend the meeting. These leaders would subsequently link up with the force at the eradication site on March 22, 2009. This included the Combined Joint Task Force Phoenix VIII (CJTF Phoenix VIII) deputy commander, Colonel Scott Thoele, and another soldier, Staff Sergeant Coventry. These leaders would join with DynCorp and CNIK ETT leaders in order to stay with the Black Hawks during the operations.

Nine • *The Black Hawks Find the Largest IED Factory*

First Lieutenant Adam Cole

"We were getting close to the end of the poppy season, and we were going to go down to Gershk, which was on the northeast side of Highway 1. We were going to spend a couple of days up there eradicating poppy. Anderson, our doc, was supposed to take leave, so they sent us another medic to replace him. They sent Anderson, I think it was to Settle, and they gave me the new guy 'cause they figured if a new guy can survive in a truck with Bill Brewer and Freddy Falmier, then he could probably survive anywhere.

"We had one more trip down to Nad Ali before we went to Gershk, and on that one Major Merseal knew I was getting a little frayed or what, but he decided to have Snacks [First Lieutenant William Sandell]

Pogue Mahone hits IED near Gershk City (photograph by Greg Strong).

The Afghanistan Poppy Eradication Campaign

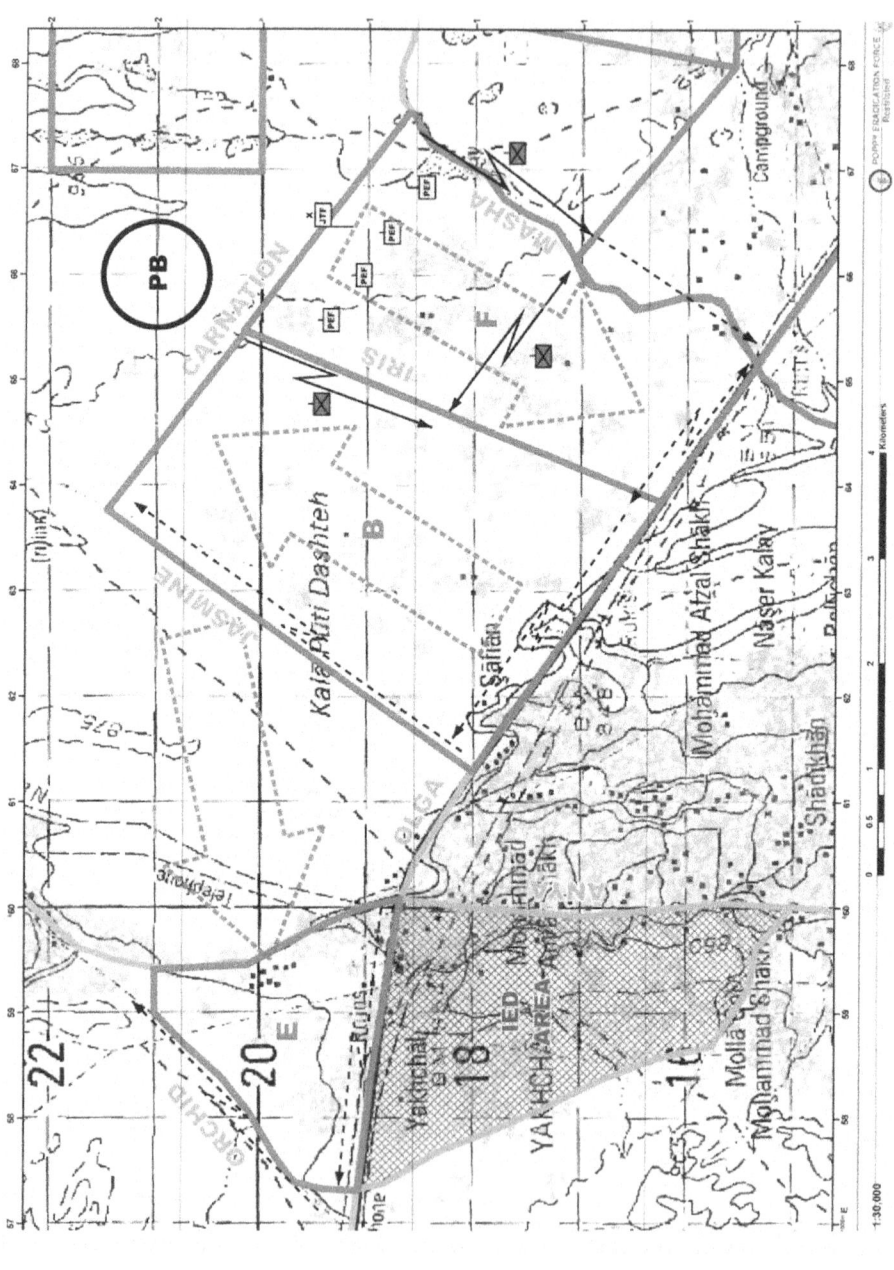

104

Nine • *The Black Hawks Find the Largest IED Factory*

and Settle go down on that one and check for the IEDs. They didn't find shit, and we took the same road, but we set up in a different position. Instead of the over-watch on the outside of the canal, we went down next to the British patrol base and set up there.

"We had this new guy, Worker, he was the new medic. I was pretty sure, since we were close to the British base, the Taliban hadn't emplaced any IEDs. I just tossed Worker the metal detector. I was like 'Check around the truck for IED's; I will be back in a little bit,' and just walk off and go check on my ANA and get them all set up. Then I go talk to the British guys and see how things were moving.

"Settle and Sandell aren't having any trouble getting set in, so I come back and Worker is scanning literally, like, two inches in front of his feet. Then he would take, like, a little shuffle step and then scan real careful, and I was like, 'What the fuck are you doing, man? Give me that damn thing.' I just scan it and walk normally, and I was like 'That's how you fucking do it.' Then I told him I was just messing with him and to go get in the truck. He gets back in the truck, and he is just sitting in the back like a passenger, and we are watching things develop.

"Settle and Sandell started taking a little bit of fire from the south, and nothing moving on us. There was a house up and to our right, and we started seeing indicators that we were going to take fire pretty soon. All of a sudden Brewer kicks off with his .50 caliber, and then he'd lob a couple 203s whenever he had a chance. He started burning through most of his 50 ammo that he had in the turret, and he yells down at Worker and tells him to get him more 50 ammo. Then he says, 'Have Bob help.' He looks down and says, 'What's wrong with him?' 'He is sleeping, sir,' Bob said. The son of a bitch had put his headphones to his little M3 radio player, and then he had the headphones on and all he could hear was music with a .50 caliber going off right above him. I said to Bob, 'Hit him.' Bob, the little polite interpreter, doesn't want to. I yelled at him and said, 'Hit him in the face.' 'OK,' Bob said and hit him in the face, and about that time Brewer kicked him. It wasn't a good start for Worker.

Opposite: **Map of operation for March 24, 2009 (map courtesy Greg Settle).**

The Afghanistan Poppy Eradication Campaign

"Anderson decided to push off his leave a little bit to make sure we still had coverage with a medic, and we took off for Gershk. I told Worker to sit down with Anderson and 'get your aid bag together and make sure it's all set.' Then Merseal had to take off because DynCorp had apparently been telling everybody that we were a bunch of cowards or something because we wouldn't fight and there were areas we wouldn't go into. The only incident they could refer to was when they wanted the ANA to go out on this mission, and they were supposed to provide water for them and were unable to at the time, but they wanted them to go out anyway on this mission in the desert in over-100-degree weather without water, and Major Merseal refused for them to do it. He said, 'That is goddamn stupid; you get these guys water,' and we delayed one mission because of it. He had to go brief a bunch of generals on what was going on and what had happened. After that we were never bothered again.

"We started pushing out to Gershk, and DynCorp tells us they are going to meet us out there. We went without them, going through the sand, and I mean it was just loose sand. Settle got out of his truck. He was stuck, and one of my ANA soldiers was riding in the back of a Ford Ranger, and one of them gets thrown out. They are, like, waving us down, and I stop and get out, and Bob or Oscar, I can't remember which interpreter was with me, and I told him to find out what was wrong with him. He was obviously in pain because two guys were holding him up. I told Worker to take care of the guy; I am going to get security established, I will be right back. I was like 'You got the terp to help you,' and so I go out, and I am shouting directions in Dari because I was really proud of the fact that I could speak the language.

"The ANA were actually getting pretty good at setting up security, and I get them set out, and I go walking back, and Worker still has his aid bag on his back and he's just, like, crouching down overlooking the guy. I was like 'Worker, what the fuck is wrong with him?' I was like 'Is he really hurt, or does he just want medication?' Worker said, 'I don't know,' and I told him to figure it the fuck out, and he just wanted medication. 'Give him an ibuprofen so he feels better, and we can get back moving.' That son of a bitch didn't even check the guy; he just gives him an ibuprofen, and we got back on the move.

Nine • *The Black Hawks Find the Largest IED Factory*

"We started moving, and Settle has another truck get stuck, and they just destroyed the transmission in the truck trying to get it out. I mean, it's done, and Sury was up in Merseal's truck up in the front, and so we get the ANA set in again with security. Settle was still back with the broken-down truck and he had the Brits. Sandell was with me, and I was like 'Well, I am going.' We go down with Settle, and Sandell is going down with me, and Sury was going to get all the security set. We still hadn't heard shit from DynCorp, and at this point we were getting real good at just avoiding likely emplacement areas on the edges of fields, staying away from the IEDs, and so we were kind of hugging the hillside.

"The hill was at an angle steep enough that I wasn't real comfortable with it, but I'd rather do that than hit an IED. We were standing there, and we get down to Settle. We had one truck that only went out a couple of times, Pogue Mahone was its name, and that's because Rabbitt was Irish and he's from Massachusetts and wanted to name it that, and we just called it the Pogue. Thorpe was helping us out, and it was him and Anderson and Foth in that truck, and we had made him a gunner, and Settle says, 'OK, Snacks, get this truck out of here. The Brits are going with you,' and I was going to stay with Settle.

"We are going to try and get this truck out, and if not, we are going to fucking torch it. They take off, but they don't take the hillside back, and they were down just a little bit closer to the fields. Snacks just missed the IED—his tire tracks were right next to the IED—but the Pogue goes right over it, and there is a hell of an explosion. We ran one hundred or two hundred meters up there, and no one was hurt. The only thing that happened was Thorpe spilled his MRE milkshake. We grabbed the metal detectors and cleared our way to them.

"Settle told the Brits and me to go back up to the other truck and burn the fucker. We are setting up security right here. I get excited— I get to burn a truck—so we take off up there, and I had some thermite just for such an occasion, and I get out an extra can of fuel, dowsing the whole thing and thermite on the engine block, and we were just having a hell of a time. I was all happy, and we finished and went back up and set into security."

The Afghanistan Poppy Eradication Campaign

March 22, 2009

A Danish recovery team arrived in the early morning at a link-up point on Highway 1 to meet with the Black Hawk Cougars Redman and Wizard, which escorted them to Pogue Mahone's location. The recovery team assessed the damage and began its operation. Prior to the recovery team's departure, the Department of State's Air Wing helicopter arrived with Major Kurt Merseal arrive to assume their positions within the patrol base. The force then established a new patrol base approximately one kilometer west of the original site.

Just as they were set up, two 107mm rockets were fired by the Taliban and impacted within the patrol base, with one approximately 75 meters from the team's position. The ANA then sent a force to clear a clot near the patrol base. The clot was empty, but one soldier noticed several suspicious items. His leaders reviewed his findings and notified the EOD, which determined that the site was a bomb-making factory, as a massive stock of materials for various types of explosives and other items were everywhere. The EOD, ANA, and Black Hawks assessed the area, and the site was destroyed.

First Lieutenant Adam Cole

"We'd made a deal with Safaris. They had a whole shitload of staff officers that wanted to get combat action badges, so we made a deal that we would take them out on a mission with us if they would take care of whatever we needed. We wanted some ICOM scanners—they are little scanner radios—and we got some of them. I told my interpreter to make sure he wrote down whatever was said over the radio. If they have any specific names, we could try and pull some shit out of this.

"We are sitting there; he is listening and says, 'This guy's on the roof somewhere and he is watching us.' I was like 'Hey, Freddy, you see anyone on a roof? There's a guy somewhere on a roof and he is watching us.' Freddy is scanning the area, and he says, 'There is a guy over here,' as he was scanning the houses. I said, 'Really?' and I was like 'Pop a

Nine • The Black Hawks Find the Largest IED Factory

couple rounds over his head and see what happens.' He fired, and, sure enough, they were on the scanner saying they could see Freddy. I told him, 'Just light them motherfuckers up.' Freddy did.

"When we pull security, we always check all the houses within our perimeter, and my ANA company was checking the area, and they got all excited about something. They had found an IED factory that created the IEDs that blew up our trucks. I go up there, hop out, and they are really excited, and I'm thinking this isn't going to be good if they are excited about something. I walk into this house, and there's 152mm Russian field artillery rounds just sitting there and mortars just lined up, and they've got, like, det cord and rubber cement and batteries everywhere, and I'm like 'I just found a fucking IED factory.'

"I was like 'All right, let's get the fuck out of here and get DynCorp EOD because I don't want any of this shit going off,' and about that time Bill Brewer comes strolling in, and he's looking around, and I was like 'Bill, just get the fuck out,' and he is stubborn, and he starts looking around, and I was like 'No, seriously, get the fuck out,' and he walks into a room and sees a little light flashing, and I said again, 'Let's get the fuck out of here.'

"EOD guys found later that the flashing light was an intrusion device. They ended up blowing the whole thing up. About that time the brigade commander had come out there, and we had a little circle of Cougars inside the perimeter, and he's sitting there, and I was like 'So, have you guys seen a fair amount of combat?' He says, 'Yeah,' and then he asked if we thought we would see anything that night. Bill Brewer says, 'Sir, if we don't get anything in the next ten minutes, we won't see anything tonight.' As he turns and walks away, a 107mm rocket impacts maybe fifty or one hundred meters from us.

"Then we were in a fight, and we start returning fire, and through the ICOM scanner we're hearing they got a guy hit and they are trying to get him out, and we are just lighting them up. I go over to check on my Afghan mortars because they are lobbing rounds. I wanted to make sure they were going out of our perimeter. I come back over and the brigade commander is standing behind one of the trucks. I asked how he was doing, and he said, 'OK,' and asked how things were going. I was like 'It's apparently great; we just hit one of them.'

The Afghanistan Poppy Eradication Campaign

"I was like 'Bob, get over here and bring your log.' He had been keeping a log of all the transmissions. Unfortunately, Bob was doing that on the back of a *Playboy*, so he brings over a *Playboy* to this full-bird colonel. A *Playboy* with a bunch of sharpie writing on the back of it. I was like, just, 'Goddammit.'

"Later in the trip we ended up in another big ass fight, and I damn near killed John Sury because we were in this long line, and I don't know what the hell he was shooting at, but either they had another AGS-17 way away from where we were, but he was shooting his Mark 19 and it was hitting close to my guys. I'm sitting there screaming at him over the radio, and meanwhile Worker's running around being stupid. We are about ready to kill him. Right after the mission Sury pulled him out of the truck because he thought we were going to kill him because the kid was worthless.

"Big fight, and nothing really happened on that one either, and we're getting ready to go into a Danish FOB and check our vehicles that are down and get some chow. We had been out there every day and been in fights every day in Gershk. Coming in, we hadn't slept hardly at all—just shy of hallucinating tired—and we're getting in, and on this weird road we're kind of boxed around, and it had a big ass ditch that they pulled all the dirt to fill up the barriers, and as we're on that road Bill's going straight, and I'm like 'getting kind of close to when he should be turning and slowing down.' I'm like 'Bill, Bill, Bill,' and he had just zoned out and went through that ditch and rolled the trailer we were hauling.

"Bill Brewer never will admit he's wrong, never! He came damn close that time, though, because there was nothing he could say—he just rolled the damn trailer, but we were just dead tired on that one.

"We got done with that, and Worker had been with us for a week at that point—maybe a little over a week. We passed back through Camp Tombstone, and we dropped him off and told him, 'You find who the fuck ever sent you to us and you tell them you ain't ever coming back.' He was gone. We got rid of him as soon as we could because he could have got somebody killed."

About an hour later, the Taliban staged a massive attack on all of the ANA positions on the eastern side of the patrol command base.

Nine • The Black Hawks Find the Largest IED Factory

The enemy fired RPGs, PKMs and small arms fire for more than an hour before letting up. All the Black Hawk teams went to the front lines of their respective companies to suppress the enemy firing positions and remained there as sporadic firing from the Taliban continued throughout the night. Department of State team members Colonel Thoele and Staff Sergeant Coventry joined Redman's crew.

Just as the Department of State members were getting into the Redman Cougar, the Taliban opened up with small arms fire. The door of the Cougar was open, and one enemy round hit First Lieutenant Troy Kemper on the cheek.

First Lieutenant Troy Kemper

"In the middle of the desert near Gershk Ali Major Merseal is having a meeting with Kandak commander, and all of a sudden we start taking fire. I am sitting in the driver's seat of the Cougar, and as Major Merseal comes in our interpreter opens the back door. He gets in, and at that instant when the door opens a round flies through, bounces off the dash, and it actually strikes me in the face, then bounces down and melts to the size of a bottle cap. All I'm thinking is 'WOW, I just got hit.' Major Merseal pulls his red flashlight up, looks at my face, and says, 'You're not bleeding—suck it up, let's go.' That was the end of it. I was like 'All right, fine, I will suck it up,' and we took off and drove to our location so we can put down cover fire.

"Then, ultimately, once we get back to where we can get out of the truck, I started looking in the floorboard and found the round. I still have that round today. I mean, it was one of those things that doesn't happen to most people—getting hit in the cheekbone by a round that bounces off. It left a red mark for about two or three days, but it didn't puncture the skin. I was truly blessed."

Although Lieutenant Kemper felt the impact and a burning sensation from the round, he did not have any injuries because of the distance the round had traveled and the fact that it had ricocheted before hitting him. Shortly after this incident, the firing stopped. At least for a while.

The Afghanistan Poppy Eradication Campaign

March 23, 2009

The plan for March 23 was to conduct eradication operations in Target Area N. The Black Hawk team moved out of the patrol base with the Afghan forces to set up screen lines in the target area. 1st Company ANA was assigned the southern screen line on Highway 1; 2nd Company had the lower portion of the eastern screen line; and 3rd Company had the upper portion of the eastern screen line. The ANP had the northern screen line.

DynCorp began the eradication operation and immediately started receiving small arms fire. One employee of the DynCorp was wounded in the leg and was evacuated. Then the 2nd and 3rd companies were attacked with heavy mortar and machine-gun fire. The firing was significantly heavier and more accurate than any previous engagement for the Black Hawk team. The mortars landed within fifteen meters of Thumper, though west of the vehicle. The firing was coming from multiple positions.

Thumper moved up to support Wizard while Redman and the JTAC vehicle assumed Thumper's original position. The Black Hawks in Redman and the JTAC vehicle dismounted and began to engage in order to suppress a PKM position. The ANA began to maneuver to the northeast, and shortly afterward all the mortar fire ceased. An F18 was on station to provide a show of force as the eradication operation concluded, and the fighters withdrew back to the patrol base without any further contact by the Taliban.

March 24, 2009

Target areas F and B were the focus of operations on March 24. Early in the morning the force moved out; 3rd Company was assigned the southwestern portion of the screen line, while 2nd Company covered the southeastern portion of the screen line and 1st Company covered the eastern portion. The force received no incoming fire from the Taliban while moving out.[3]

Nine • The Black Hawks Find the Largest IED Factory

Shortly after the force was in position and the eradication operation began, a 107mm rocket was fired at the War Pig, hitting the ground and tumbling onward as it approached. Fortunately, the round didn't explode.

First Lieutenant Adam Cole

"One of our last missions we found some IEDs, took a couple mortars and small arms fire, but it wasn't no big deal. We grabbed a couple of locals, and we weren't supposed to interrogate them—we weren't supposed to tactically question or interrogate anybody—so I just started a conversation with them. I was like 'Hey, you guys from around here?' and the interpreter is like 'He said yes.' 'OK,' I said, 'where do you live?' and they point to a house. I was like 'OK, what's the name of that guy that lives in that house?' as I pointed to one. They had no clue. Well, I know damn well you don't have a TV, so you damn well know who your neighbors are. We just sat on those guys all day and then let them go when we were getting ready to leave. We didn't have any way to haul them, so we left it up to the ANA if they wanted to do anything with them, and they let them go.

"We started seeing activity right after that as we were leaving because it is their favorite thing to do, because they claim victory because they drove us off. As we were leaving, I see a bullet magnet—it just flashes from this house—and they had fired a 107mm rocket right at Settle's Cougar, and it hit something before it got there, and it hit the dirt and tumbled and stopped about one hundred meters in front of his Cougar. It was right in line with his truck. The EOD had to blow it up."

Shortly after that, the Taliban opened fire on the eastern screen line with small arms and machine-gun fire. The ANA returned fire, and about ten minutes later the firing stopped. The EOD team then conducted a controlled detonation of the 107mm rocket in place. With the eradication operation complete, the screen lines were collapsed and the force moved to the new Patrol Base 2. Colonel Thoele and Staff Sergeant Coventry were transported to FOB Bastian and later flew back to Camp Phoenix.

The Afghanistan Poppy Eradication Campaign

March 25, 2009

On the morning of March 25, the Black Hawk team, ANA, ANP PEF, and DynCorp moved into Target Area D. 2nd Company ANA took the western portion of the screen line; 1st Company maneuvered into the southern portion of the screen line; and 3rd Company covered the eastern portion. On this day there was no contact from the Taliban.

As odd as it might seem to outsiders, when soldiers are used to being in fire fights every day, and then there is nothing to do but sit and scan the area, the men often start getting bored.

Sergeant First Class Greg Strong

"Sometimes we joked on the intercom; some guys took downtime and just chilled and rested in place or took a small nap. It was weird because the ANA knew when we were about to get hit. You are watching your sector, but you are watching the ANA because one minute you are looking around, you see them lying down half asleep or asleep, and you are on the radio or relaxing, and then all at once you see them all postured up, ready to fight. I mean, it was just that fast, and you knew it was coming. There is something about them. They have this instinct that we could never figure out. I guess if all you know is fighting, it comes as an instinct, but they were right every time.

"For me the downtime in the field wasn't relax time. I couldn't relax because I knew it was going to kick off—I just didn't know when. I stayed in the turret most of the time, and I did have a little swing seat that I would sit in from time to time, but not very often because I couldn't trust anything around me."

Then there was the game playing. One might say that boys will be boys.

First Sergeant John Sury

"We used to play games with the British air controlling team. It was getting stupid, and that is where we were getting dumb: playing games, putting MRE milkshake bombs under their trucks. We would do it while they were eating lunch. It would blow up, and they would

Nine • *The Black Hawks Find the Largest IED Factory*

start running around thinking they had been hit by mortars. It kept building up, and we would booby trap their Humvees.

"The MRE bombs are made by using the heating element out of the MREs. We would take that and put it in a plastic bottle with water and shake it. When the heating element started heating, it would blow. It was just water but sure made a loud sound when it exploded.

"It finally came to a head one day. We put them under one of their trucks while they were eating lunch, and it blows up. It pissed them off, so they started throwing their MRE bombs at me. They run up and throw them on the truck, and I am getting milkshake all over me. It was actually water, but I was soaked.

"There were four or five of us standing at the back of the truck just horsing around. We did that when we weren't having any fire fights or activity because of being bored. The Afghan commander had been telling us all day to move back, we were in a bad position, and we kept telling him, 'No, we need to be here so we can see down to the other line.'

"Out of nowhere we had a machine on us, mortars, and RPGs. An RPG came right over our heads and exploded about ten feet behind us. Everybody is just scrambling, and shit was blowing up all around us. We couldn't get in the truck by the passenger door because the machine-gun fire was hitting all over the side of the truck on that side. Major Merseal came around with the truck so we could get in on the driver's side. While I was waiting for one of the guys to get in, it was just like in the movies. I can see the bullets coming at me in the dirt, just eating it up, and I am standing next to the truck, and the bullets are hitting about six inches from me, and I am thinking I am going to die. He got in, and I finally scrambled and got in the truck.

"We had a AT4 antitank rocket in the center console, so we got it ready, and one of the guys says, 'I'm going to get out and shoot this thing.' He opens the door, and something came by and hit the mirror. I don't know if it was an RPG or bullet or what, but it took the mirror off the truck, and you could hear the bullets hitting the side. He shuts the door and says he can't get out on that side. He looked at me and said, 'You want to do it?' I said, 'Yeah, I'll do it.' The machine gun was about 150 meters right in front of us. I get the AT4 and set the sites, and I get out and run behind the Brits' Humvee. I check everything,

The Afghanistan Poppy Eradication Campaign

and by now the Afghans are shooting. And Captain Settle's truck is behind us, and his Afghans are shooting RPGs from way back, and they are hitting near me. I fired the shot and got them on the first round. I ran back to the truck, and we had another AT4 strapped on the back of the truck, and I got that and ran back and set it. I fired it and hit close, but they were already done.

"One of the Brits had an AT4 and yelled and asked if I wanted to shoot it; 'It keeps misfiring on me.' I said okay, so I went over and I tried it. Click, and I re-cock and fired again, and click. I tried one more time, and just as I got it down a little it fired. The rocket went about 50 yards in front of us and went off. Man, that's when I realized I didn't have my ear muffs or my headset from the truck. Man, I couldn't hear forever. My head hurt, my ears were ringing, and I am in a daze. After a while it stopped. After that we never played any more milkshake games."

First Lieutenant Adam Cole

"Major Merseal freaked out when he got shot at by an RPG; it was the first time he had come under direct fire, and he screamed like a girl on the radio, and it was the only time I've ever heard him that unnerved. I thought, 'Somebody got hit at first.' Then I realized nobody was hit, and I just realized he was panicking—he'd had his window shot out because he was out fucking around playing pranks on the British guys.

"I am sitting there, and I just look at the other guys in my truck. I was like 'Oh, Jesus, I don't sound like that on the radio, do I?' and they're like 'No, you sound bored.' I was like 'OK, good, I just wanted to make sure.'"

Captain Greg Settle

"We had been down in Helmand Province for quite some time and were getting toward the end. We had been in about one hundred fire fights and some really good ones. We were pretty seasoned at the time, and we were going to go on one of our later missions. I remember the boss man Kurt says, 'Why don't you take the west side on this mission?' We looked at the map and the terrain, and there is no way we'll get hit from here. One of those exact nothing going to happen side. I

Nine • The Black Hawks Find the Largest IED Factory

noticed he had placed his truck right in the middle, which I would appreciate if something was going to happen. That was the plan.

"We establish a screen line; it was around noon and was usually around the time we would get attacked if it was going to happen. We picked up on some things going on: people were moving around, some of the women and children were leaving some buildings. I saw the boss pull his truck out a little bit and push forward just a little bit, and I said, 'Hey, boss, what are you doing? You may want to back up a little bit.' He says, 'No, no, I'm just giving them a target to shoot at.' I was like 'That probably isn't a very good idea.' He goes, 'Oh, I got this.' I was like 'OK, all right.' Well, nothing happened for a little bit. Everyone is sitting around, and all of a sudden the bad guys unleashed on us.

"They just pinned his truck down, and fortunately at the time we were a very disciplined group. I don't know what happened at that point in time, but Merseal and Sury and Campbell and a couple Brits were playing grab ass outside the truck, doing what they weren't supposed to be doing. I remember an RPG went by and blew a mirror off his truck while Kurt was trying to get in it. Then he gets on the radio and starts screaming like a little girl, 'They are shooting at us, they are shooting.' We started laughing and said, 'Yeah, we see that, why don't you scream back?'"

Sergeant First Class Jeffery Sowash

"We were out at Gershk on a mission, which was always hairy because they had a lot of buildings, which gave them a chance to take a lot of shots at us because of better concealment for them. We had a Raven, which is a remote-control aircraft with a camera on it, so we could see what was going on. Garcia was flying it and he was bringing it back, and as it was coming in everything was looking perfect. Then I remember Garcia saying, because I was in the gun most of the time and Garcia or Jimmy would be driving (later on it would always be Garcia because we got ahold of a .50 caliber and Jimmy is sniper qualified, so we gave him the turret, and there's actually, besides the regular gun turret, there's another hatch, and so Jimmy and I would

The Afghanistan Poppy Eradication Campaign

both be up there—he would have the turret and I would have the M-19).

"The Raven is coming in, and everything is looking perfect; Garcia goes, 'Everything went dead.' The Raven just kept going right past us, and we were watching it, and it just kept going, kept going, kept going, and it was way out there, away from where it was supposed to be. We are trying to figure out how we are going to get it back. We were told we couldn't go past certain limits. We knew the only way we were going to be able to get it, since it was past the limits, was if Major Merseal didn't know we were going after it.

"If we went, we had to shut the blue force tracker off so Major Merseal couldn't track us. I look at Jimmy and the lieutenant, and we say, 'Shut that thing off.' He did, and they immediately start calling us on the radio. We drove about five or six thousand meters, and the Raven had crash landed and is broken all to hell. We get all these parts packed up and drive back to where we were supposed to be. We turned the blue force tracker back on and said on the radio, 'Oh, we got it figured out now. We were just having some issues with it.' I don't know to this day if anybody knows what we did other than me and the guys with me. Although it was broken all to hell, we didn't lose the Raven. We figured it could be repaired.

"We would get bored out on patrols, and Lieutenant Sandell (Snacks), he always blamed it on being a latchkey kid. He'd come home from school every day when he was a kid and his parents wouldn't be there, and he'd watch *Star Wars*, and he could literally recite the entire *Star Wars* movie—every single line, every single part, including the characters that don't speak English—from start to finish. If we were bored, Jimmy and I would say, 'Hey, Snacks, let's watch *Star Wars*,' and for the next two hours he would recite the entire script of *Star Wars*, doing every single character, and he would do Chewbacca in character. He would do his own character; he had the entire thing memorized. We listened to *Star Wars* probably ten times while we were out there in the desert. We also played word games on occasion to pass the time."

After DynCorp had completed the eradication operation, the screen lines were collapsed and the force returned to Patrol Base 2.

Nine • *The Black Hawks Find the Largest IED Factory*

March 26, 2009

The last day of the six-day operation focused on Target Area M. The Black Hawk team, ANA, ANP PFE, and DynCorp moved into the target area. 1st Company ANA took the eastern portion of the screen line, while 3rd Company took the northern portion and 2nd Company monitored the southern portion of the screen line on Highway 1.

Once again there was no enemy contact from the Taliban, and following a successful day of poppy eradication, the force collapsed the lines. After returning to Patrol Base 2, the Black Hawk team moved to FOB Price to escort Pogue Mahone to FOB Tombstone/Bastian for repairs.

The Black Hawks then returned to FOB Eagle. They had completed their mission. Not only had they destroyed several fields of poppy, but they had also found and destroyed the largest IED factory in Afghanistan.

Ten

The Last Days

> "The last mission was kind of mixed emotions because your senses are heightened. No one wants to be done in on the last day out on a mission." —Sergeant First Class Greg Strong

April 3, 2009

It was early morning and a hot 100 degrees. The Black Hawk team was preparing for another mission, loading supplies and checking ammunition, but their minds weren't on the heat. This was their last mission in Afghanistan. By this time, they had been in more than 100 fire fights, and now it was almost over. Unsurprisingly, they were nervous. If they could just get through this one, it would all be done. No one wants to get wounded or killed at any time, but the last mission brought extra pressure for everyone. On this day, they weren't saying much—just loading the vehicles and hoping they would return to FOB Eagle when the mission was over in the Cougars and not a body bag.

As they had done so many times, the Black Hawks were going on a joint operation with the ANA CNIK, ANP PEF, and DynCorp in an assigned eradication area (target areas K9G, K9H, and K9K, south of Nad Ali, north of Marjah, and west of Khoeshhal Kaley within the Food Zone). This operation was the second of three planned missions back to the Food Zone. The original plan had called for this operation to take place on April 2, 2009, but it had been rescheduled because of severe wind, sand, and rain storms. Previous operations in this area of

Ten • The Last Days

the Food Zone were conducted in Nad Ali, and the force had experienced significant enemy contact (AK-47s, PKMs, RPGs, mortars, ZSU-23s, and 107mm rockets) with one friendly KIA (ANA CNIK).

This operation would include men from two large and well-resourced anti-coalition forces. The forces from Battle Group Center South (from the United Kingdom) had conducted shaping operations in Khoeshhal Kaley previously; they requested that firing within that area be measured and that positive identification be made to reduce collateral damage.

The Black Hawks would conduct a deliberate combat operation to establish two support-fire positions and seize and hold three objectives (a series of structures/clots located with three geographical areas within the larger target). The concept was based on a ground reconnaissance conducted by the force two days prior. Once in possession of the three objectives and providing security, the ANP PEF would execute their eradication operations.

The Black Hawks performed an SP from the FOB to break their old pattern of departing and made a tactical move to the fire positions in order to seize the objectives before the enemy was prepared.

The Redman team included Major Kurt Merseal, Captain Mark Foth, First Sergeant John Sury, Sergeant First Class Sean Rabbitt, Major Kurt Walser, and interpreter Mirab. Those in War Pig were First Lieutenant William Sandell, First Lieutenant Brian Mays, Sergeant First Class Greg Strong, Lieutenant Colonel Paul Moreno, Lieutenant Colonel Michael J. Schuh and interpreter Zabullah Safi. The Wizard team included Captain Greg Settle, Sergeant First Class Jeffery Sowash, Staff Sergeant James Ressel, Specialist Kegan Anderson, Captain Quincy Springs, and interpreters Ahmad Noor and Mustafa Noori, while Thumper had First Lieutenant Adam Cole, Staff Sergeant William Brewer, Staff Sergeant Freddy Falmier, Staff Sergeant Kyle Campbell, Private First Class Zachery Tyminski, and interpreter Haroom Ahmed. A British contingent (JTAC) moved with the force for additional support and traveled in a HUMWV for better protection; First Lieutenant Troy Kemper traveled with them as a driver and the Black Hawks' fires support officer. They moved behind Redman and, when in the fire positions, they placed themselves close to Redman to provide

The Afghanistan Poppy Eradication Campaign

communications to close air support (CAS) assets. The team was being jointly led by representatives from General McKierman's office (liaison to the U.S. Embassy), Lieutenant Colonel Moreno, CSTC-A ANP, Lieutenant Colonel Michael J. Schuh, and the ARSIC-S, Major Walser, in order to provide assessment of operations to their leaders.[1]

The Kandak's executive officer leading the operation ordered the 1st Company to seize Objective One and, when able, to push a platoon or platoon-plus-sized force to an area south of Patrol Base Sijab on Phase Line Foster to prevent enemy forces in Khoeshhal Kaley from projecting into the battle space. The 2nd Company was ordered to cross the canal after Objectives One and Two were seized and conditions had been set for them to maneuver along Phase Line Foster prior to seizing Objective Three. This would prevent the enemy from maneuvering against forces from the south and east. The 3rd Company was ordered to seize Objective Two, simultaneously with 1st Company taking Objective One, in order to prevent the enemy forces from occupying that area and projecting into a battle space.

The Black Hawks would provide a support-fire position, with two MRAP Cougars (Redman and War Pig) stationed west of the canal to provide over-watch within the area and direct the CAS assets. The British JTAC, combined ANA mortar teams, and an attached EOD team would be positioned at this point. The team's other MRAP Cougars (Wizard and Thumper) were located in the support-fire position on Phase Line Foster occupied by the platoon from 1st Company. The Black Hawks would also provide a dismounted force (Captain Greg Settle, First Lieutenant Adam Cole, Staff Sergeant William Brewer, Staff Sergeant James Ressel, Staff Sergeant Kyle Campbell, and Specialist Kegan Anderson) to mentor the 2nd Company as they seized their objectives and to provide force protection.

The lead mentors for 1st Company (Captain Greg Settle) and 3rd Company (First Lieutenant William Sandell) switched command of their trucks, as the 1st Company lead advisor was assigned as the EET commander on the ground in order to provide the team chief with immediate information. The 1st and 3rd companies would operate without their respective mentors directly with them.[2]

Ten • The Last Days

As the 1st and 3rd companies deployed across the Canal Zone, the Taliban opened fire on them with small arms, and two 107mm rockets landed behind Redman and War Pig but did not detonate. Once the 1st and 3rd companies had secured their objectives and 1st Company pushed a platoon to establish the support-fire position south of PB Slab, the decisive operation shifted to 2nd Company.

2nd Company established a foothold and established the support-fire position over-watching Objective Three. As they moved, 2nd Company and the dismounted force began to receive enemy small arms fire from the northeast in the vicinity of Khoeshhal Kaley. Once they had secured Objective Two, the Kandak's support-fire position west of the canal bore the brunt of enemy small arms fire that continued throughout the operation.

As the three objectives were secured, the ANP PEF began to occupy the eradication area and initiated eradication operations. Small arms fire continued at all three of the Objective positions and two support-fire positions. The Department of State's Air Wing (DoS Air) received enemy small arms fire and (anti-aircraft ZSU-23) from an area south of the 1st Company advising team's position. Although the Taliban continued to fire at the aircraft, they often shifted to the support-fire positions and the ANA objective rally point, with rounds landing or air bursting within fifty meters of the vehicles. As the DoS Air aircraft maneuvered to avoid being hit, Major Merseal called in AH-64 Apaches, F-18s, and an armed Predator to destroy the enemy force.

As the force prepared to collapse the positions, mortars and sporadic anti-aircraft guns were fired, with rounds impacting approximately seventy-five meters in front of Redman.

Sergeant First Class Jeffery Sowash

"We had to convoy back, and we got into several fire fights. They always liked to hit when we were leaving, made them think they were running us off, but we hammered them and hammered them good with everything we had with us. During that point in time it was very nice."

As the CNIK moved from its objective rally point, the ANP PEF began to receive fire from the ZSU-23 to the south. The enemy was soon crushed, and the force moved back to FOB Eagle.

The Afghanistan Poppy Eradication Campaign

The Convoy Back to Kabul

The mission was now over. The men were excited. No more poppy eradications or watching for IEDs and fire fights. It was time to pack up.

Sergeant First Class Greg Strong

"The last mission was kind of mixed emotions because your senses are heightened. No one wants to be done in on the last day out on a mission. Then, once we got back, it was like the weight was off our shoulders. We just got to make it through the night, and then there was the two-day convoy back. We didn't have the Taliban going to hit us every day like we did on daily missions, but it was scary until we actually got back to Kabul.

"The morning after the mission we tore down the tents and burned everything we didn't need. It was semi-sweet and kind of a celebration. That night came a rainstorm, and so it was windy and just hell, but we were still excited. Then we started back, and we had an escort come up and meet with us. It was funny because some of the escort was guys that were in our battalion. Day one went great. Day two we were going, and we had stopped. It was like a piss stop—everyone had a chance to go. We had a ridge line on our right, and one of the guys asked Brewer, 'Hey, do you think we will get hit?' Brewer looked at him and said, 'You sit anywhere long enough and you're going to get hit.' It wasn't a minute later that a 107mm round came in and exploded.

"We got back in our trucks, and there happened to be like a valley in the ridge line, and we backed up and pulled in there. There was a clot that they had fired from, and we just lit that bad boy up. We had a perfect fix on the clot because we were on a hill and shooting down. We just tore it up, and that was the last fire fight we had going back, but also the last fire fight we would be in. That night we pulled into Kabul. We were a happy group of men."

First Lieutenant Adam Cole

"I mean, it was just a God-awful up-and-down thing, and then by the end we were just so emotionally drained and stressed and just on

Ten • The Last Days

a hair trigger. I lost it on the way back. We stopped at Kandahar and I was okay, and we were going to stop at FOB Warrior Ghazi, which I spent my next deployment at not even a year later.

"We stopped in, and Bill and Freddy were driving, and I had been telling them, 'Hey, guys, we are staying the night here,' and they're like 'no, no, no.' They said this because Sury was fucking with us, saying we were going to sleep in our truck. I was like 'No, we are staying here,' and they were being stubborn, like they had the whole deployment. It wasn't anything beyond what I had dealt with, but I just lost it.

"Once we got into the fucking FOB I just started screaming at them. Settle had to grab me and pull me away because me and Freddy were going to fight. He was going to kill me, and I mean he is a lot bigger than I am and a lot meaner. It took me about twenty minutes to get calmed down, and I went over and apologized to Freddy. I said, 'I don't know what happened to me,' but it was just, we were all so keyed up. We just sat there, just built it all up. We all had little moments. I saw Kyle Campbell, one of the nicest guys in the world, he about went after Willy one day. Willy was being dumb, but I mean he just fucking lost it, and we about had a fight.

"When we got back up north we had this sergeant major, and he was a real asshole. He told Major Merseal we were all going to have to stay in one B-hut together. Would have been really crowded, and Major Merseal did a very smart thing. He told the sergeant major, 'You do realize, if you put all these guys, keyed up as they are, in one little confined space like that, they are going to lose it? They are going to kill each other, or they are going to tear this fucking place apart. These guys need some space, and they need time to get depressed.' He didn't care.

"We ended up taking our damn tents down to Camp Julian instead of Camp Dubs and set up our tents. Now we are living in our tents again, but we had our space and nobody bothered us. It was the best thing because we had about a month by ourselves because the ANA went on leave, and they were gone too.

"I went home on leave and literally went from Helmand Province and fighting to my parents' house. My brother's kids are running around, and it was just a weird transition. I just didn't feel real

The Afghanistan Poppy Eradication Campaign

comfortable, but the month or two that we had by ourselves helped us all decompress. We got back and moved all over the place. Mays got out. Snacks moved to California and transferred out of the Guard. Troy Kemper moved to Nevada and then back to Illinois. I ended up bouncing around; I was a scout platoon leader when we got home, and then I got bored and decided to volunteer for another deployment. I came back from that one, and Settle roped me back in and said, 'Hey, we might get deployed again; we need you to be a company commander.'

"I came back to be a company commander, and then deployment went away, and I'd passed up one job in Colorado because I thought my guys were going to deploy, and I wasn't going to stay home while my guys got deployed. Then got another job out in Colorado as active-duty assistant S3, so been there ever since. Then got married, and now I have a kid on the way."

After leaving Helmand Province, the men were happy to be in Kabul, but it was a difficult adjustment. There had been fire fights every day up to this point, and even in the FOB there had been a constant concern that someone could be hit. Now, however, it was quiet. Not sometimes—all the time.

Sergeant First Class Greg Strong

"The decompression from combat is kind of uneasy. You have all this quiet, and you're not used to the quiet. You're either balls out or asleep out there. It was wake up, load the truck, go out and fight, and come back, clean the weapons, and then sleep. Then get up, load the truck, and go out and fight, and it was like that every day. All of a sudden you have all this downtime. You really don't know what to do with yourself.

"The first couple of days were rough, but then everyone started working out and started getting their minds back right. It was weird, getting three squares a day, because that's something we didn't have for a long time. It was decompression time, but it didn't prepare us for when we got back to the civilian world. It's just not the same. People don't look at you the same. They ask you what you did, and when you finish telling them they have this 'what the fuck?' look on their face. They want to understand it, but they can't grasp it. That is why a lot

Ten • The Last Days

of veterans stay together. Our team has stayed together. We all talk, and we are close to this day."

The Black Hawk team remained in Kabul for a couple more months, decompressing and resting up. They had been in well over one hundred fire fights; they had experienced multiple close calls; they had discovered the largest IED factory in Afghanistan; and they had provided security under heavy fire on most days so that DynCorp could harvest 11.2 tons of poppy seed. And although the CNIK team before them had lost half its men, the Black Hawks were returning home unscathed. Maybe it was their training, or luck, or God looking over them (or perhaps a combination of all three).

Eleven

Five Years Later

Steelville, Missouri, located in the foothills of the Ozark Mountains, is surrounded by rolling hills and clean running streams (namely, the Meramec River and two spring-fed creeks, Yadkin and Wittenberg). Sixty miles southwest of St. Louis, Steelville has been called the "Home of Hospitality," "Floating Capital of Missouri," and "The Population Center of the U.S." It is also the home of Major Kurt Merseal.

In September 2014, I was invited by the Black Hawk team to come to Steelville for their annual reunion. I arrived on a Friday evening, taking the winding roads out of town until I saw a large sign with an arrow: CNIK. A mile or so down the gravel road, there was another sign for turning into the driveway. As I drove down the hill and then back up the hill, I wondered whether this counted as a Route 1; it was more like a road than a driveway. What seemed like a mile later, I came out of the woods into large opening. In the center was a beautiful log cabin home where Major Merseal lived.

Over the course of the next few hours I had the privilege of meeting eleven members of the team. For the remainder of the evening, I watched as they met, drank and reminisced. They were no doubt a true band of brothers, with a bond that only comes from serving together in combat. During my stay I interviewed each one of the team members. Here are some of their reflections and comments about their experiences in Afghanistan.

Eleven • Five Years Later

Major Kurt Merseal

"I guess the first thing is organization of the team. We had 16 slots on a team—most of them senior NCO or junior officers, supposed to be captains and majors. We didn't have enough captains to go around, so we ended up with lieutenants, and some of them were junior lieutenants, to fill the captain spots. On the NCO side, we should have had E-7s and E-8s, but we filled the positions with E-6s and E-7.

"When it came time to organize, we had to do a balancing act because there were so many teams that had to be filled. We had to hand-pick our team, and most of our team was out of the Midwest—some from Missouri and most from Illinois. We went to Fort Chaffey for four weeks of training, and we had the autonomy to do basically what we wanted. We put a training plan together with real simple principles. And we did a ton of shooting. We shot till we had blisters on our hands, short range and long ranger. We also did a lot of first aid and survivability-type stuff and communications. After two weeks there, we went to Fort Riley and went through training, learning how to be combat advisors, and continued on marksmanship, communications, and language skills. That's when we learned what our mission was going to be.

"Once in Afghanistan, we wouldn't just fly from the seat of our pants. We wouldn't do a brigade-level combat operation into a town like Marjah, which was arguably one of the worst towns in the country at the time, with no planning, so there were several times we put the brakes on. We shut down the entire operation through most of the time in Afghanistan. We would mentor Afghans in the planning process, and I would say, 'We are not ready to go; you need to complete this planning process.' We wouldn't tell them what to do; we mentored them and let them decide, so we built a good relationship and they listened to us. After several times of that, it made it back to the embassy. I had a general and some other senior officers, both from the U.S. Embassy, but the British embassy also, that was on my ass because the Afghans wouldn't do what they wanted. The general agreed with me in the long run that diplomatic ambition wasn't going to override military principle, and so, instead of doing things by the seat of our pants,

The Afghanistan Poppy Eradication Campaign

we started using military decision planning and command, which went along with the mentoring we had been trained with so that the Afghans could do the job as they were supposed to instead of us doing it for them.

"I could go take a bunch of monkeys and go knock down poppy all right, but to teach somebody how to do it is a different story. I told you it was my theory about what this thing was about. The United States had irrigated the area back in the 1930s and had created this tremendously fertile farmland for the Afghans. It was a bread basket for Afghanistan. Then, after we disrupted the structure after we first invaded, the Taliban, who was very strong in Helmand Province, took control. They turned all this fertile farmland into a bread basket and started producing opium. The Taliban were getting 47 percent of their funding from opium. American was kind of looked at by the world community as creating the conditions for this, and considering most of the opium was going to Europe, something had to be done by the United States to correct the situation that they had created.

"Most of the days were very similar. We would go through the planning process after the PEF would determine where they wanted to eradicate the poppies. We would do our planning, and we would get our Afghans and we would come up with a plan. One of the problems we had was when we would give our Afghans the graphics and the map; no doubt there was, and we think it was the intelligence officer, we pretty much nailed down on it that he was working for the Taliban. We would roll into an area—supposedly nobody had a clue where we were going—and there would be IEDs laid in our graphics. I mean, it was perfect, and I was amazed and very impressed with the Afghans' ability to read the map when we struggled to teach them how to do it, but somebody could read the maps, and they could put IEDs exactly where the over-watch positions were going to be.

"On a typical day we would go out and assign a truck with each Afghan company. I would provide over-watch again, and we weren't commanding, but in a sense we did kind of orchestrate a lot of what they did. We tried to let them make as many decisions and do as much as they could, but at times it was required that we'd have to step in. One thing we did was provide direction fire support and the air

Eleven • Five Years Later

coordination, so we orchestrated the combat multipliers that kept the Afghans alive and allowed them to do their jobs.

"We would go in a large area and secure three sides, and the PEF would put the easy side where we had just come from. Most days we would set in, and in a short time we would start having contact. Sometimes it would be tense all day, and other days it would be lighter contact, but it was not if you were going to get hit, but just how long was it going to be before they set in on our positions and we had contact.

"We would sit there and start getting hit with RPGs, PKMs, and machine guns, and even at times they shot anti-aircraft guns. They shot our version of the Mark 19—it was the AGS-17—and we took some pretty good hits, but we were really lucky: none of our team got hit. But the Afghans took some hard hits.

"The typical day was just go out and clear an area, and some days we would be in contact all day long, and others weren't quite so bad. After a while, though, we would start getting sloppy. Unless they got real close, we didn't even worry about it. I had a little stove, and we would fire it up and make tea, and unless the pinging got real close we wouldn't stop drinking our tea.

"You never quite knew which direction the bullets were going to go, and not that the Afghans would intentionally do it, but sometimes we would go out on operations, and we would do extended operations basically, and we just lived in the middle of the desert just outside of the irrigated area; we just set up a perimeter and dug in old-school style, just out in the middle of the desert, and that's where we based our operations from. We basically set up there because we were out of rocket range. They would shoot at us all the time, but to have good accurate shots they would have to come out in the desert with us. That would make it more difficult for them. We would leave there and go multiple days or maybe a week of operations, and then once we were done we would come back, and wherever we were, we would set up a semi-circle in a place we could defend easily, and we would have Afghans on one half of the perimeter, the Afghan police on the other, and put our trucks in a box in the center of the perimeter. That's kind of how we lived. Just sleeping there on the ground, and I'd say it wasn't a bad life. It was actually kind of fun, camping throughout Helmand

Province. I never heard anyone bitch about it. Morale was good on the team.

"I really took to heart the training of the Afghans. Our training facility was Helmand Province, and we were always trying to figure out the enemy, always trying to figure out Afghans better, always trying to develop them, always trying to develop ourselves, and there were days that we would just push up a little bit, knowing that we were going to get into contact, but we did just for the sake of 'let's see what the enemy's going to do; let's see how long it's going to take them to make their move on us.' When you start thinking of a training plan where there are live bullets coming at you, hard training is important. If I lose an Afghan or if I lose one of my guys, it wasn't going to be for the lack of training. It is really worth it, but on the flip side of it, it's like, if you don't do this, and when we roll into Marjah and we are fighting our ass off, what do you have then without good training? We pushed the training pretty far, and it paid off. We never lost any of our team and a few Afghans, but it could have been a hell of a lot worse."

Captain Greg Settle

"We're sitting here roughly five years later, trying to recall some of the things that happened, and as time goes by you forget some of the actions on ground or some experiences, but everyone remembers specific things that they bring back with them. We did our reunion last year, and a majority of the individuals on the team were still there—that's what was amazing. We went as a group and did what we did and accomplished what we accomplished under very challenging circumstances. The team we replaced had a 50 percent casualty rate, whether wounded or killed in combat. For us to take everybody over there and come back with everyone is quite remarkable. I don't know how much of it was luck or how much of that is skill. I think it is a combination of both.

"There were days when we were down in the valley or down in Nad Ali and Marjah area, and I remember being out on point, just guiding, doing what you do, and looking around and thinking, 'We aren't all going to get out of here today.' I mean, you look at the terrain,

Eleven • *Five Years Later*

you look at what your mission is, and would think, 'We are going to get into it today, and we are going to get into it good. It is going to take a good bit of luck for us to all get out of here today.'

"Most of the guys on our team were veterans. A lot of them are police officers and are gun savvy. We had expert shooters and stand-up infantry guys, and everybody took pride in their ability to shoot. And I remember we were sitting somewhere, and a Taliban had come out of the back of a building. He had shot at us and was running out of the building with his gun in hand. Then there were four of them shooting at one of our guys. They missed. That just doesn't happen, but I am telling you it did happen. Where I started to go is that we are all still here.

"We don't talk to each other as much as we probably should, but we were such a tight team, and to bring everyone home intact is almost impossible. It's about taking care of our soldiers and making sure that everyone is okay. I know for quite some time, once or twice a year, I would call everybody and asked how they were doing. 'How's your wife? How's your children? Hey, let's get together and go fishing.' When you have been on a team that has gone through what we went through, no one else understands. No one can really relate.

"I've deployed 3 times, 2 complete deployments in Iraq and then this one. I had a fairly easy deployment in Iraq. I don't know how many people we have deployed in Operation Freedom and Enduring Freedom, but there are many that have gone through what we went through. There are units and groups that had challenging circumstances, and for so many to go out there and come back with a good attitude is amazing. This team is the real deal. We had a few Bronze Stars, but the motto on our team was 'we don't hand out awards.' Major Merseal made sure of that. He said, 'You're in the infantry; you will get shot at and you will shoot back, and that's your job. If you want to get an award, you're going to earn it.'

"When you go through combat, you experience every emotion known to man—happy, excited and sad, the full spectrum. But I do appreciate what all the guys on the team did. I've had my life saved several times, so I owe them a lot. They are truly great Americans. I was honored to serve with them."

The Afghanistan Poppy Eradication Campaign

First Lieutenant Brian Mays

"I first found out that we were going to do a joint operation with the Afghanistan National Army and the National Police to help eradicate poppy in the fields of Afghanistan. I was thinking, 'What does that mean, right! What is poppy?' I didn't know, but come to find out you can make heroin and other drugs out of it. I felt I am going to go over there trying to take something of value to a country that uses it to export across the world. My first thought was 'We are going to be in contact with the Taliban and take fire from them, and we are going to be firing at them. You are going to do something different that is exciting, but scary at the same time.'

"In Kabul at the first base, we got to know the Afghan officers and NCOs and got to know their structure. After getting to know them, we felt better than just getting thrown into a mix going in to combat. It was very cold in Kabul, which is contrary to belief, because you think you're close to Iraq, so you thought it would be just hot. It made it incredibly difficult, because you had to carry around so many different types of clothing, but we left Kabul and went down to Helmand Province in a four- or five-mile-long convoy. We stopped in the desert in the middle of nowhere. I remember asking Settle what we were doing now, and he said, 'This is where we call home for the next four or five months.' I tried to wrap my head around it: just stop in the middle of the desert, and this is home. But days passed and bulldozers started building barriers, and we started establishing a foothold in the middle of nowhere.

"I remember talking to some of my friends that went over there to Iraq and even Afghanistan, and they said, 'Oh, I guarded a FOB,' or 'You know, I went on a few missions here and there, but we never saw contact.' And they would ask about me. I'm like 'Well, every day we went out was a surprise.' I mean, literally every time we went out of our makeshift FOB, within hours of where we were supposed to be we were taking fire. I mean, we were a big target, and we were taking away money from the Taliban, so that was a key component.

"I don't talk a lot about my experience over there, contrary to what my brother did when he came back. He felt like, when he came back from Iraq, he had to broadcast his experiences. Not in detail, but he felt he was due something from the civilians back here for what he did. I remember telling him, 'You volunteered for the army. You made that choice. You knew you would potentially go overseas and fight. It came with the deal,' and he could never really grasp that.

"When I came back I had a good job waiting for me. I had a family that was very supporting, and so it made it very easy for me to get back and adjust myself to society. Contrary to where he was, but he had just got out of school and was very young. I was a little bit older. He was an NCO E-5 sergeant, and I was an officer. Rank doesn't matter, but maturity, I think, helped me benefit in adjusting and moving on."

First Lieutenant Adam Cole

"I've been a platoon leader for like two years, been working with those guys getting ready to deploy, and Captain Settle was actually my company commander at the time. He calls me about two weeks before we were supposed to mobilize, and he's like, 'I got a great opportunity for you.' Anytime Settle said that, it was a terrible idea—something bad was going to happen to me. He is like 'We are specially selecting you to be on this team; we are short, and we need you.' I'm like 'OK' and said goodbye to my guys. They weren't too happy about it, since it was only a short time before mobilizing and I had trained with them.

"We were at our going-away ceremony, and Settle told me that Merseal was heading up the team. I knew him by reputation; everyone had something good to say about him, so we know we are going to have one hell of a team. I see him on the steps outside the building we had the ceremony in, and since Settle said I was selected and everything, I thought I ought to go say hi and tell him I appreciated him picking me for the team. I go up, and I was like 'Hey, sir, just wanted to thank you for picking me to be on your team.' He just looks at me, and he goes, 'Oh, you're on my team?' That is how I got started with the team.

"Shortly after that we went to Fort Riley to train up for this whole thing. We went to headquarters the night before we left [for Fort Riley], and I was good buddies with Willy, and we decided to go out drinking the night before we left. We almost got kicked out of a bar, Karaoke night. The next morning I'm trying to get Willy up; I'm trying to get him to go catch the bus, and he says, 'I'm going to drive.' I told him he was too drunk to drive, and I ended up driving 6 hours hung over to Fort Riley, Kansas.

"Once we were at Fort Riley, it was honestly the only time I was in the army that we played by the no-shit, big-boy rules. They gave us our class times, and Merseal had a good PT program. We got in the best shape we had ever been in our lives. We drank more than we ever drank, and we bonded as a team.

"We still didn't know where the hell we were going, and we found out like right before we left, like we were going to take over some other counter narcotics infantry EET. We didn't have a fucking clue what that was going to be. We thought we were going to go out to western Afghanistan, where nothing went on the whole time, and all of a sudden we get this dropped in our lap.

"We get over there, and we are at Phoenix, and Merseal sets out to find the guys we are going to replace. We go to Camp Dubs, and Merseal finds the team we are replacing and talks to them. He comes back and just looks beat down, like the wind just got taken out of him. He said, 'We are fucked; they had 50 percent casualties on their team.'"

First Sergeant John Sury

"I was the senior enlisted man on the team. We got our mission, and we arrived in Afghanistan and finally met up with our replacements. That was probably the most shocking thing that I saw there. Just the look on the guys' faces—it was just unbelievable. They were just done, and it took us back. We knew we were in for a real interesting mission down south. The movement down, living like animals living in the desert, the rain and cold.

"What I want to talk about is the dynamics of the whole thing. What intrigued me the most was the massive interaction between us as army advisors to the Afghan army dealing with the DynCorp

Eleven • Five Years Later

contractors and the poppy eradication force and the Afghan police force, and just how we all kind of interacted? Then, in addition, we had the State Department that was running the whole show.

"Major Merseal and myself would go around and try to put some sense into this and try to keep from doing stupid missions that would kill us and the Afghan soldiers (and probably them too). We put a stop to a lot of stupid missions, but we had our ups and downs with it. These officers through the State Department would come up with missions, and we would tell them that we were just advisors and we didn't tell the Afghan soldiers what to do. We are here as advisors, and we aren't calling the shots.

"It came to a head one day when they wanted us to do a mission in Marjah area, where there was a Taliban stronghold. They said we are going in and eradicating poppy, and we told them our Afghans told us that it was way too dangerous. We told them that we couldn't do this type of mission because the Afghan government had assigned us and the Afghans as a support unit, not a direct combat unit to clear villages from the enemy. Also, there were too many civilians in the area that would be injured or killed. DynCorp accused us of being cowards. This stirred up a whole mess at the State Department.

"It was me and Major Johnson, the S-3 officer who was at the briefing when the mission was coming down. The Afghan religious officer was the first one that stood up and said, 'You know we can't do this. This is not in our orders to conduct such a mission for a combat operation.' So they kept accusing them of being cowards. We have the DynCorp contractors and the State Department representatives yelling at the Afghan officers. It was just out of hand, and the representative officers yelling at the Afghan officers that they were cowards, and finally the religious officer jumps up and starts yelling back at them and says, 'Hey, look, we aren't scared of anything; if you can get our government to authorize it, then we will do it. We are not scared of killing anybody. We will make the village safe if our government okays it.'

"This went on and on, and they kept picking at the Afghans, which was something that we avoided doing. We tried to build trust while we were there because we depended on these guys for protection. We never disrespected them; I wouldn't stand for it. Early on, if I did see it, I would nip it in the bud if one of our guys said something or yelled at one of them.

"Finally, I stood up and just started yelling back at this guy. I'm like 'No, you do not understand what he's saying. He is saying they are not going to do it,' and we just got up and walked out. That stirred up the pot, and we got visitors from the higher commands and everywhere else trying to influence the Afghans. It was a no-win situation, and eventually we did go in, but it was just the whole political turmoil that surrounded this whole operation with so many elements involved.

"We did our part; basically, that was it. We just did what we could. It probably built the trust with the Afghans and prevented problems with us. You hear the shooting, and that went on when we were in Kabul. We did have a threat of a suicide bomber from within our own ANA Kandak, but he was caught at the gate coming in. The Afghans arrested him. They kept us informed about things, and we had built that trust and rapport with them, and had we not, I don't think they would have cared about us and our safety.

"We had two meetings with the United States Embassy over the actions our Afghan soldiers didn't take. That is because the State Department representative had gone back and said we were refusing to do missions. Major Johnson, Major Merseal, and myself stood by our guns and just told them, 'We are advisors. We are not commanders of the Afghan army.' They couldn't get it in their heads. You hear about the Afghan army being incompetent, but overall these guys would have done the job, and they protected us all the time, and we counted on it. They were the main element of the operation, and that always intrigued me.

"As for the Black Hawk team, we all made it out of there alive—lucky, I guess, because I don't know how we did it."

Sergeant First Class Greg Strong

"When we first got to Afghanistan we went into this B-hut, and there's this major from the other team that we were replacing, and we asked him, 'Hey, what's the rules of engagement?' He said, 'By God, it's whatever you can live with,' and we were looking at each other like 'what the fuck is he saying?' When he was done, Major Merseal met with us. He said, 'That's bullshit, boys. I'm telling you right now, we are following the rules of engagement. Boys, whatever you can live with, we're going to do within the proper perspective of life. Don't be murdering anybody, but whatever you can live with; if they're shooting at you, man, you just tear them apart, let it go.'

"We were at Riley first, and then we got to Kabul at Dubs when Major Merseal gave the speech. We had been on ground for a day or two, and we're doing 'left seat, right seat' with the other group. Greg got up there, and he says, 'OK, boys, we are going on a dangerous mission, so look to your left and look to your right, because one of those boys aren't coming back.' That was right after he found out the team we were replacing had lost half their team. That's when the pucker factor really set in, but I think going into it with that in mind, it helped us all.

"It's an experience that I wouldn't change for the world. I wouldn't trade anyone that was on that team. It's something where talking to you is probably the most I've talked about it other than with Greg Settle, 'cause a lot of people don't understand it, and by the time you explain what you're talking about, they kind of lose interest in what you're telling them. People just don't get it. Vets know, but other people just don't.

"Watching Brian Mays and Greg Settle, it was impressive watching them move the day they threw the grenade in the bunker. And the day they had to go get one of the ANA that got his melon split by the Taliban. It was bad; he was a good soldier. He was a real good soldier, one of our hardest fighters. He walked around the corner, and the Taliban stuck an AK right at his temple and blew half of his head off and then put four more into him to make sure he was dead.

"You know, there is a lot of good stuff and a lot of bad stuff, a lot of death. I would be lying if I didn't say we used every ounce of prayer, every ounce of nine lives, every ounce of prayer from home and every ounce of luck. There were so many close calls that could have went the other way, and we all came back unscathed. I mean, just one inch the other way and there are several of us that wouldn't be here. If that 107

The Afghanistan Poppy Eradication Campaign

had hit the chicken shield—that's the shield in front where your gun sits between on the turret—it would have blown me in half. Hell, if it had even hit the front of the truck, even though the windshield is 6 panes, it would still have penetrated and would have damaged us and rattled around pretty bad. We just had a lot of close calls."

Staff Sergeant James Ressel

"I think the biggest thing about the beauty of this was that no one in our team was hurt. As many fights as we were in, direct contact, and close calls, someone should be dead or seriously hurt. One of my best friends was killed in southern Afghanistan. He was on a force protection mission, just driving convoys back and forth from Kandahar to wherever someone needed to go. He was blown up when his truck hit an IED. He never fired a shot there and is IED dead. It just is really strange how things work out. We went, I think, in a 9- to 11-day stretch where we were in direct fire. I never felt stressed or upset or disturbed by it. It was just what you did: get up in the morning and go to work. Poor guy, Josh Melton, there's a memorial to him down in southern Illinois at one of the wineries. It's in Greenville, and my buddy Adam Cole had his wedding reception there, and it was the first time I had seen it. I didn't know it was there, and it brought back a lot of things home. I am not good with emotions; I just kind of push them to the side. Josh was a great friend of mine, and I loved the guy. I got to see him about four times before we got all split up on different teams. Two other dudes in my platoon were killed about five klicks from where we were at. I'm not going to say there is a master plan, because I don't believe anything of the sort, but it's just strange—people you were close to are just not there anymore.

"In our Kandak we did things that were just ridiculousness. It's hard when you have hard-headed individuals and ones that don't speak the same language, even with an interpreter. The big difference between Americans and Afghans is, for example, we would get briefed by Major Merseal on what we needed to do that day: 'You got to get A, B, and

Eleven • Five Years Later

C done.' We would go to the Afghans, and they would say, 'No, we have ten first.' Then we have to talk for at least thirty minutes before we start. Americans want to get it done, and we would say, 'Hey, we got to get A, B, and C done; we are rolling in ten minutes.' It was difficult mentally because they just worked differently than we did. They are more social there and much more hospitable than we are; they're savages and barbarians, but they are very polite and nice people down to the core. It would take them thirty minutes to agree to what you told them ten minutes ago. 'No, we not do that today.' We would have to go around with them so they didn't lose face that we told them what to do and let them come up with the idea that you had briefed them on forty-five minutes ago after seven cups of tea and a pack of smokes.

"I really don't have any bad memories from there; I really don't. We shot some people and hurt some people, but I don't feel bad about it, never had a bad night's sleep, never had a nightmare.

"I remember Kyle Campbell and I were sitting on a rooftop one day, and a mortar came in. The mortar landed, seriously, went down the side of the wall by my feet. It missed me and Kyle by about a foot. The only reason we didn't get hurt was it hit the wall and slid down and detonated on the ground. A lot of people, especially when we got back, would say, 'Oh, you had a close call; you almost died.' I never looked at it that way; I always looked at it as I am still alive. I never looked at it from a negative way. My dad always taught me not to dwell on the negatives. Hell, I came home with all the parts I left with, and I'm thankful for the experience. I would do it again.

"One of the best things about this team is how funny everything was because we joked around a lot. It was just a really unique dynamic that was in the group that we have, and the best thing about the boss man, Major Merseal, he knew exactly how to get 100 percent out of each one of us. He understood exactly what motivated and knew what it took to get the most out of his people individually. I mean, tactically, he's the best officer I've seen, hands down. Captain Settle's really close, but for being a redneck from Steelville, Missouri, he is sharp as a knife. He is the best officer I have ever served with, and I have been doing it for eighteen years."

The Afghanistan Poppy Eradication Campaign

First Lieutenant Jason Williams

"We knew we were going over, and I was supposed to go over as a platoon leader. Two weeks before we went to Fort Riley, I get a call from Captain Settle. He says, 'I want you on my team; get your shit together, we are going.' I was in the police academy and thought I would be able to finish, but I was wrong. I told my buddies at the police academy I would see them in a year.

"I headed for the headquarters where we stayed the night before we left for Fort Riley. A friend of mine talked me into going out to drink that night. I was going to drive my truck the next day, but we got really, really drunk, and I got kicked out of a couple of bars. I was so hung over the next day that Adam [Cole] had to drive the truck to Fort Riley.

"At Fort Riley we would train, shoot and whatever the day required. Get up and PT. At the end of the day we would go back to the barracks and drink beer. We did everything together. We would go fishing, hunting, hung out together as a team, building that cohesion. I got along with everyone, although a couple of guys would piss me off once in a while. Then they told us what our mission was: the narcotics mission to eradicate poppy. I think our success as a team came from what we learned at Fort Riley and our cohesion as a team. We all had each other's backs."

Staff Sergeant Kyle Campbell

"Before our deployment to Afghanistan, I was a staff sergeant in Headquarters Company for 2nd Battalion, 130th Infantry. I was a fire support sergeant. I was a 13 fox; I wasn't an infantryman. I was an artilleryman doing forward observer work. I had just finished the Joint Fire Observer School (JFO) at Fort Sill. I can call forward direct and adjust any indirect fires at my disposal, be it mortars or artillery, and then the training was in how to call and direct any close combat attack from attack helicopters or close air support from the jets. I don't know if that's what got me into the team or not, because I was the only one

Eleven • *Five Years Later*

in the battalion that had that training. I had already had a deployment to Iraq, but I was a mortar man then. They were hurting for men to go to Afghanistan and asking for volunteers, so I volunteered and said I would go and got selected for the team.

"I met up with everyone at Fort Riley. I knew Kurt Merseal from before in Iraq, but I only knew him as he is the company commander for Charlie Company, and I hadn't really been around him much. I didn't know the other guys in the team till I met them at Fort Riley. While we were there we built close bonds pretty quick, which was nice because it helped us later when we got to Afghanistan.

"I said earlier I don't know how I got picked for the team or I don't know how the team came together, but we had an incredible team. It was a really good bunch of guys. Maybe I'm biased because I was part of the team and I was with those guys, but if it was anyone else, I don't think it would have turned out as well. We had a really good crew and an incredible leader. I would follow Kurt Merseal anywhere, hands down. He had a way of getting the best out of every man.

"While there I was really afraid of the IEDs. In Iraq that was all they used. That was their weapon of choice. They wouldn't stand toe to toe and fight because they had lost too many times, so they wouldn't do it. That was one of the greatest appreciations in Afghanistan. They would come out and fight—win, lose, or draw—and go toe to toe with us, and it never worked for them, but they would keep coming. It was almost therapeutic for me after having gone through Iraq and all the IEDs and all the trucks we lost. When one of our trucks would get hit in Iraq, we would go into a rage. It was frustrating because a truck would get hit, and they were trying to kill our friends, but there was nothing you could do because there wasn't anyone there. In Afghanistan it was different; the bad guys would come out and try to kill you, but you got the opportunity to try to kill them back.

"Our job was to protect the DynCorp so they could eradicate poppy. The Taliban would fire back and come toe to toe with us and start shooting from the clots. We couldn't go after them because it would leave the DynCorp people unprotected, so we would just fire back and get them in a group of clots, and then blow them up with air power. If we could have shot through the walls around the clots, we could have handled a lot more of the situations without air support, but I never once felt vulnerable.

"I had an opportunity to do a lot of really great things, but in no way does that make me great. I can't look back on any day or any instance and say that, yeah, it was a decision I made or an ability of mine or some kind of skill I had. All the credit goes to the team; without them, it would have been a lot different."

First Lieutenant Troy Kemper

"Part of my mission was keeping up with the personal records, documents, and awards—all the paperwork. Half of my job was mentoring the Afghan National Army, my counterpart. It was interesting, interacting with the culture and understanding some of the different personalities. I took on a kind of spiritual leader role, so the team knew I was praying for us. While there I did a Bible study with a couple guys, and it helped me get through a very stressful and trying time, and the guys had respect for that. The guys I deployed with, I would trust with my life today."

From Troy's Diary

August 8, 2008

God, thank you for watching over us as we traveled from Marion to Fort Riley today. Thank you for watching over Karl, Isabella. JAK father continue to watch over, protect, provide for and comfort my family. Help Keri to ask for help from friends and family. Help me Lord to follow you where you are leading me. Help me follow you one day at a time and not worry about tomorrow. Use me as your tool/light for my ETT team. God I am thinking about a prayer group weekly devotional. God help me just to put me out there for the team. Whatever I do let it be in your will. Thank you God for truths that you have shown me through experiencing God and continue to guide me close to you and your will. Thank you for loving me as your son. I love you God.

Amen

August 18, 2008

God Thank you for watching us as we traveled from Marion to Fort Riley today. Thank you for watching over Keri, Isabella, and JAK. Father continue to watch over, protect, provide for and comfort my family. Help Keri to ask for help

Eleven • Five Years Later

from friends and family. Help me Lord to follow you and not worry about tomorrow. Use me as your tool/light for my EET team. God I am thinking about a prayer group and weekly devotional. God just help me put myself out there for the team. Whatever I do, let it be in your will. Thank you God for the truths that you have showed me through experiencing God and continue to guide me closer to you and your will. Thank you for loving me as your son. I love you God.

Amen

August 20, 2008

Yesterday I completed the SRP process. I only had to receive the PPD, typhoid, Anthrax, and small pox vaccinations. Really both my arms are feeling pretty good. Every once in a while I can feel where they gave me the typhoid and anthrax shot they gave me in my right arm. This morning I got up at 5 a.m. and did a cardio work out and got a new ID card. That's all for now.

Today "Day 3" has been the longest day yet. Today started off fine, but after getting the ID card have had nothing substantially to do. I cancelled that insurance, contacted CALL for information on Afghanistan, read the bible, and did my quiet time. But after that I have had all afternoon and evening to do nothing and I worry tomorrow will be more of the same. And the 4 day weekend is cancelled.

August 21, 2008

I worked out with Bill this morning and we had a good talk about his beliefs/religion. I will continue to talk with Bill. Bill is a new Christian and seems to be on fire for God, but not too strong in his faith. Hopefully with God's help I will be able to assist Bill in strengthening his faith so that he can become a better witness to Christ.

August 23, 2008

It is Isabella's 4th birthday today. She is such an amazing little girl. Keri is doing a great job of raising her in the Lord. I am so proud of both my girls (Keri & Bella). I know Keri will continue to serve God and I will try lead/push her in order to help her grow.

Isabella, sorry daddy missed your birthday party. Know that I miss you, I love you, that I am very proud of you. You are a brilliant (that is a fancy word for smart) little girl and you are the best big sister to JAK.

Daddy

August 24, 2008

Dear God,

Dad—Dear God let your will be done in his health condition. I asked that you heal him only if it is in your will.

The Afghanistan Poppy Eradication Campaign

Mom—Give her strength, Lord. Strength to carry her through while I am away.

Tiffany—Watch over her and Nat, God keep them both safe through the upcoming C-section.

Mike, Max, and Bradley—I pray for their salvation. I pray they will all have an intimate relationship with you God, through your son Jesus Christ.

I want to pray this same prayer for Tammy, Kane, Tim, Carol, Zach, and Johnny. Lord I do not know each of their hearts, but I pray that they all would accept you as their Lord/Savior.

Keri—Lord give her strength to be a single mother to Isabella and JAK. Support her, comfort her, calm her Lord until I return home.

Lord keep Isabella and JAK safe Lord and let them know how much I love them both while I am gone.

August 28, 2008

God,

I sat through a brief this afternoon where the CG "1 Star" talked about our mission and why our class was not getting a 4 day weekend for Labor Day. The reason he gave has stock in it. The reason we are not getting the 4 day weekend is because we are training for WAR! "If you have a problem with this you need to get your priorities straight."

I am going to war in 2 months. God help me get mentally, physically, and emotionally ready. Keep me in your word and your will Lord. Help me be the rock for my family and watch and keep them safe.

Today Keri called about break problems, not being packed yet, and overall stressed out. God calm her nerves and give her patience with Isabella. Let her know that I love her and will always love her. I am so proud to be able to call her my wife. Help her God. Please! Thank you for sending your son to die on the cross and to rise from the dead 3 days later just so I could be saved, God. Thank you. I love you.

Amen

September 5, 2008

I am working hard this week to get into your word. I am starting to read 1 Kings. My major distractions this week has been all the evening studying that is required. This week we have been learning the Afghanistan Culture and the history of Dari. This week we have also been in CPL Settle's PT program. Yesterday we participated in a cultural meal sitting on the floor eating a common Afghan meal on the floor with our hands. I also learned that one of the cultural specialist's brother was in an IED attack in August. He had hurt his back and has no feeling from the waist down to his knees. Please God heal him physically Lord. God I am going to be learning a lot of new information CLS to advance Dari to

Eleven • Five Years Later

combat service and support. Lord let me be a sponge and absorb all that I can so that I can be effective as possible winning the hearts and minds of all that I come in to contact with on this mission.

September 11, 2008

I have been on title 10 orders 4 weeks tomorrow. So far I learned Dari. After last night's class, it looks like this will be self-taught language until I get in country. Yesterday I passed the written and hands on test for combat life saver. Today we sat through IED class. I am reading 1st Kings. Eli died this morning after hearing the Ark was taken from Israel. The more information that we are hearing about the west, the more I get concerned. It sounds like everybody is getting into shape and staying focused on the mission, but at night and on weekends, the guys are getting drunk, partying like they were in college and going to strip clubs. God, help me be your light in these times of darkness.

November 18, 2008

We arrived at Kabul around 6 a.m. today. We were bused from the airport to Camp Phoenix where we grounded our bags and went straight to the mess hall.

Around noon we left in a convoy to drive through Kabul to go to the COIN (Counter Insurgency) Academy. From the COIN Academy we can see the King's Palace and Queen's Palace. Also, the mountain range that surrounds us is amazing.

Every person that we talk to about Helmand we get the "ohh ... really?" One person called it "the heart of darkness." One of the Special Forces MSG stated he was attacked 179 out of the 180 days down in Helmand.

The elevation here is kicking my butt. 6000 feet above sea level.

Camp Julien–COIN Academy from the waist down.

November 23, 2008

Yesterday we conducted drivers on the MRAP Cougars with the team we are replacing. The MRAPs drive like a big rig. Also while the 2nd group was driving around one French soldier was killed from an anti-personal mine. He was blown up from the waist down. A second Frenchman was critically wounded. I found out today that the 2nd French soldier lost his leg.

I talked to mom today. I told her she had nothing to worry about. Then I made it back to my room and a mortar/rocket hit camp. One went off and one was a dud.

Anti-personal mines are marked all along the road on the way up to the firing range. These are the same mines that are mentioned above (killing the Frenchmen).

I talked to dad, Tim, Zach, Kane, Tiffany today. They were having Thanksgiving dinner today

The Afghanistan Poppy Eradication Campaign

November 25, 2008

Today we went to the range again. We fired the M-2 (50 Cal) and the Mark 19 (M-19). We were shifting targets (rocks) 100 meters to 2000 meters and lighting them up. Everyone on the team shot well. As we were leaving mortars landed about 300 meters from our position.

Just another reminder that we are at war.

December 12, 2008

Our mission is simple. Train the ANA Kandak to be able to travel to and defend a piece of land so that the PEF can destroy or eradicate the poppy fields in Helmand. The PEF wants to clear out over 10,000 acres of poppy. Tomorrow is when our training starts. Three days of processing then train, train, train.

A side note: 75% of the world's opium comes from the first area where we are going to eradicate.

A quote from Major Merseal, "We are given a shit sandwich and we are supposed to make it taste as good as we can."

A quote from SSGT Reed, "We are going to poppy/opium heaven and our job is to kill God."

Keri I miss more than you can imagine. I love you. Lord keep Keri, Bella and JAK safe. Give them strength to get through in the day and rest at night.

January 6, 2009

Dear Isabella and JAK,

You are both going to be great. You are my daughter and son. Not only will you be great, you will be extraordinary. I am so proud of all that you have done and all that you will both do.

Both of you love God with all your hearts. Love and obey your mother and do the best at all you do.

I love you both, Isabella and JAK, more than you will ever know.

Your proud and loving father

Dad

January 26, 2009

Well today God was keeping me safe. I was driving the Cougar from FOB Dylan to Lashkar Gah. There were times that I was sure I was going to slide right into a canal. On the bright and cheering side I did get to pull down a concrete pole and pull a cougar out to a ditch. Unfortunately, when we were recovering the 45 degree Cougar, one ANA soldier was shot in the arm. He is fine. FOB Dylan was hit by a 107mm rocket.

We are staying the night at Lashkar Gah and the food is excellent. Tomorrow we escort back thirty more tractors to use to eradicate poppy.

Eleven • Five Years Later

One cool thing is that when I see a shepherd herding sheep or look at the mud complexes/ houses, I think how biblical these people are. I mean it is like I am in biblical times.

March 3, 2009

I returned from leave last Thursday. On Wednesday when we landed in Kandahar there was a Ramp ceremony for 4 soldiers killed in an IED attack. It was a real eye opening moment to realize that "I was back in the war." Thursday and Friday were both down days. Saturday and Sunday I can't remember, but the first mission once I was back I was put on Lt. Sandell's cougar "Wizard" as the turret gunner. First day got in a tick (fire fight). Shot the M-19. We had shots within ten feet of our truck.

Don't worry baby those fire fights haven't been that bad for me.

March 14, 2009

Sweetie here are a few things I should not tell you.

1. Every mission I go out on I am always looking for someone trying to kill me.
2. I also look for PID so I can fire the M-19 at the enemy.
3. I have had small arms PKM, RTG 107 rockets and 82mm mortars fired and within 25 meters or less of me. (Truck was hit.)
4. I have returned fire with the M-19.
5. I volunteered to go out pull security on a down MI-17 helicopter.
6. Keri—these last pages are for you to read if God calls me home.

July 12, 2009

We just found out there is a strong possibility that we will be going back to Helmand. Only about 2 weeks before out processing and leaving Afghanistan.

A couple guys keep me up all night being loud and stupid.

Can't sleep all day. I'm tired and cranky.

Now there is talk of going back to Helmand where it is 120 degrees and daily fighting.

Will someone please just kick me in the balls. Please it is all that is missing.

July 14, 2009

Well as of today I am not going to Helmand on advance party. 12 more days and I get to start my journey home.

God is good.

The Afghanistan Poppy Eradication Campaign

"I actually enjoy going back to the armory; there's less of us that have deployed now in the units, so there's fewer people telling stories now. It's always fun to hear the different stories and different perspectives on things. Someone is always trying to up one on somebody else. It's fun to throw out "I was shot. Anyone else shot?" Then the stories start.

"It was definitely a life-changing moment that I have been able to apply. I've been in stressful situations: being shot at is very stressful; having other people's lives in your hands is very stressful. The experience has helped me put things in perspective with my civilian job. I mean, you go to work and you provide for your family, but from one standpoint you know no one is going to die. Things can wait for a day, although people think they can't. It is easier for me to relax.

"I think I had a very even-keel personality the entire time we were over there. During the highs and the lows my behavior was exactly the same in fire fights, and I tried hopefully to calm others down in stressful situations. It was definitely a life-changing experience, but the one big regret I had was I had to miss 9 months of my newborn's life and my oldest child's life."

I left the reunion on Saturday evening. As I pulled my car out, the team members were together having some target practice, once again evincing the strong bond that only comes from serving in combat, embodying the true meaning of "I got your back." The one thing that I can say about these men is this: I served in the U.S. Marine Corps for ten years, including two tours in Vietnam, and I have never met any greater warriors than the men of the Black Hawk Counter Narcotics Infantry Kandak Embedded Training Team, 2nd Battalion, 130th Infantry Regiment, Illinois National Guard. Each morning when Americans rise, they should say a prayer and thank God for warriors like these, because it is thanks to them that we live in the greatest nation in the world as free people.

Appendix

Black Hawk Team Members

Name—Position—Original Unit

Major Kurt Merseal, Team Chief, HQ, 2-130 IN
Major Nick Johnson, S-3, JFHQ-IL
Captain Gregory Settle, CO, Mentor, D/2-130 IN
Captain Quincy Springs, S-4, Mentor, IRR (assigned at Fort Riley, Kansas)
Captain Mark Foth, CO, Mentor, IRR (assigned at Fort Riley, Kansas)
First Lieutenant William Sandell, CO, Mentor, HHC/2-130 IN
First Lieutenant Brian Mays, Asst. CO, Mentor, A/2-106 CAV (RSTA)
First Lieutenant Adam Cole, CO, Mentor, D/2-130 IN
First Lieutenant Jason Williams, Asst. CO, Mentor, C/2-130 IN
First Lieutenant Troy Kemper, S-1, Mentor, HHC/2-130 IN
First Sergeant John Sury, Senior NCO, Mentor, D/2-130 IN
Sergeant First Class Gregory Strong, NCO, Mentor, HHC/2-130 IN
Sergeant First Class Jeffery Sowash, NCO, Mentor, HHC/2-130 IN
Sergeant First Class Sean Rabbitt, NCO, Mentor, A/1-182 CAV (RSTA)
Staff Sergeant William Brewer, NCO, Mentor, B/2-130 IN
Staff Sergeant James Ressel, Asst. NCO, Mentor, HHC/2-130 IN
Staff Sergeant Freddy Falmier, Asst. NCO, Mentor, HHC/2-130 IN
Staff Sergeant Kyle Campbell, Asst. NCO, Mentor, HHC/2-130 IN

The following individuals were assigned to the team while in theater and for the specified date of assignment:

Appendix

Name—Position—Dates of Assignment

Major Carter McReynolds, Previous Team, 29 November 2008–28 January 2009

Specialist Nathaniel Rowton, Medic, 24 December 2008–2 February 2009

Private First Class Michael Garcia, Raven Operator, 27 December 2008–7 July 2009

Private First Class Zachery Tyminski, Raven Operator, 27 December 2008–25 July 2009

Captain Anthony McLean, Medic (Army Nurse), 4 February 2009–28 February 2009

Major (Dr.) Robert Bailey, Medic (Neurologist), 26 February 2009–12 March 2009

Specialist Kegan Anderson, Medic, 26 February 2009–7 July 2009

Staff Sergeant William Thorpe, Human Resource NCO, 1 March 2009–5 April 2009

Specialist Jason Worker, Medic, 13 March 2009–27 March 2009

Thomas Koontz (USAF), EOD NCO, 29 March 2009–4 April 2009

Matthew Blough (USAF), EOD, 29 March 2009–4 April 2009

Mason Messick (USAF), EOD, 29 March 2009–4 April 2009

Ryan Milliken (USAF), EOD, 29 March 2009–4 April 2009

The following are the National Afghanistan Army interpreters assigned to the team:

Abdul Shakir	Mahammand Suhrab (Suhrab)
Ahmad Samir (Sam)	Mihrabuddin Ibrahimi (Rock)
Ahmad Seair (Oscar)	Mustafa Noori (Moose)
Haroom Ahmed (Bob)	Ramin Barack Darokhan
Jamshid Anwary (Jay)	Zabhullah Safi (Pure Clean or PC)
Mahammad Noor (Noor)	

Ordnance Expended

What follows is the most accurate record of the Black Hawk team's ammunition expenditure while operating in Helmand Province. Due

Appendix

to high operational tempo and loss of documentation on at least three known operations, this listing is incomplete. These numbers only reflect the CNIK ETT and the CNIK or other members of the joint force.

Weapon/Ammunition—Type—Expenditure

M-2, Machine Gun (.50 caliber), 12,000
MK-19, Grenade Launcher, 1,857
M-240B, Medium Machine Gun, 7,000
M-249, Light Machine Gun, 1,150
M-4, Carbine Rifle, 1,200
AT4, Light Anti-Armor Rocket, 8
Grenade, Fragmentary, 2
40mm, Grenade, 200
M-107, Sniper Rifle, 50
M-9, Pistol, 17
82mm, Mortar (ANA), 300

The following ordnance was expended under the direction of the CNIK ETT by Close Air Support assets:

Weapons/Ammunition—Type—Expenditure

1,000-pound bombs, 2
500-pound bombs, 4
2.5-inch rockets, 23
30mm, 600
Hellfire missiles, 6
Gal 77 (7.62mm), Mini Gun, 100,000
105mm HE, Artillery, 54
105, Smoke, 14

Seized Enemy Contraband

Thirty-nine Taliban fighters were killed and fourteen detainees were taken by the CNIK. Based on reports from various sources (radio and television, ICOM chatter from local Taliban fighters, and Afghanistan National Security Forces means), the number of enemy fighters killed was probably closer to one hundred fifty, with two of them (Khadahari and Mullah Abdullah) being local Taliban commanders. Of the fourteen detainees, one was suspected to be a high-ranking fighter, as his cell phone contained recordings of him delivering various speeches.

Appendix

The CNIK also was highly successful during its operation in Helmand Province in destroying approximately 11.2 tons of poppy seeds and discovering an IED factory. The factory housed an immense store of bomb-making materials and explosives that were linked to the IED strike against one of the team's vehicles (Pogue Mahone). It was suspected that the factory was not only linked to a number of IED strikes in the area but also the largest single factory in Afghanistan.

Casualties

CSM Abdul Hadi, HQ, WIA (wounded in action)
Shams Ullaq, 1st Company, KIA
Aman Ullah, 1st Company, KIA
PSG Lal Mohammad, 1st Company, KIA
Kazada, 1st Company, WIA
Zahbullah, 2nd Company, WIA
Sergeant Farid Allah, 2nd Company, WIA
Alam Moden, 3rd Company, WIA
Nazer, 3rd Company, WIA
Sergeant Qahaj Shah, 3rd Company, WIA
Idi Mahammad, 3rd Company, WIA

The CNIK ETT was involved in more than one hundred combat operations over the course of its deployment. During the seventy-five days in which the team operated in Helmand, forty combat operations were directly related to the eradication mission. Thirty-one of those forty operations involved direct engagements with enemy forces for more than fifty continuous hours. Typical engagements by the enemy involved AK-47s, RPGs, PKMs, and 82mm mortars; several also included 107mm rockets and a ZSU-23 anti-aircraft gun. In addition to the many rocket attacks launched against the force while conducting the eradication mission, 10 rockets and an unknown total of mortars were fired on FOB Eagle. The force successfully detected four improvised explosive devices (IEDs) that were neutralized by the DynCorp EOD team. One IED strike with no casualties or injuries destroyed the right front wheel on the MRAP Cougar Pogue Mahone.

Appendix

Members of the CNIK ETT received the following awards:

Bronze Star Medal with Valor (3)
Bronze Star Medal (20)
Army Commendation with Valor (1)
Army Commendation Medal (10)
Combat Infantry Badge—2nd Award (1)
Combat Infantry Badge (13)
Combat Action Ribbon (10)
Combat Medic Badge (2)[1]

Chapter Notes

Chapter One
1. Department of the Army, Counter Narcotics Infantry Kandak Embedding Training Team (CNIK ETT), Camp Dubs, Darulaman, Afghanistan.

Chapter Two
1. Counter Narcotics Infantry Kandak Embedded Training Team (CNIK ETT), Serious Incident Report (SIR) for Troops in Contact (TIC) on February 1, 2009, page
2. *Ibid.*
3. *Ibid.*, 2.
4. *Ibid.*, 3.

Chapter Three
1. Counter Narcotics Infantry Kandak Embedded Training Team (CNIK ETT), Serious Incident Report (SIR) for Troops in Contact (TIC) on February 16, 2009, page 1.
2. *Ibid.*, 2.
3. *Ibid.*, 3.

Chapter Four
1. Counter Narcotics Infantry Kandak Embedded Training Team (CNIK ETT), Serious Incident Report (SIR) for Troops in Contact (TIC) on February 21, 2009, page 1.
2. *Ibid.*, 2.

Chapter Five
1. Counter Narcotics Infantry Kandak Embedded Training Team (CNIK ETT), Serious Incident Report (SIR) for Troops in Contact (TIC) on February 24, 2009, page 1.
2. *Ibid.*, 2.
3. *Ibid.*, 3.

Chapter Six
1. Counter Narcotics Infantry Kandak Embedded Training Team (CNIK EET), Serious Incident Report (SIR) for Troops in Contact (TIC) on February 28, 2009, page 1.

Chapter Seven
1. Counter Narcotics Infantry Kandak Embedded Training Team (CNIK EET), Serious Incident Report (SIR) for Troops in Contact (TIC) on March 3, 2009, page 1.
2. *Ibid.*, 2.

Chapter Eight
1. Counter Narcotics Infantry Kandak Embedded Training Team (CNIK ETT), Serious Incident Report (SIR) for Troops in Contact (TIC) on March 11, 2009, page 1.
2. Counter Narcotics Infantry Kandak Embedded Training Team (CNIK EET),

Chapter Notes

Serious Incident Report (SIR) for Troops in Contact (TIC) on March 18, 2009, page 1.

Chapter Nine

1. Counter Narcotics Infantry Kandak Embedded Training Team (CNIK EET), Serious Incident Report (SIR) for Troops in Contact (TIC) from March 21 to March 26, 2009, page 1.
    2. *Ibid.*, page 2.
    3. *Ibid.*, page 3.

Chapter Ten

1. Counter Narcotics Infantry Kandak Embedded Training Team (CNIK EET), Serious Incident Report (SIR) for Troops in Contact (TIC) on April 3, 2009, page 1.
    2. *Ibid.*, 2.

Appendix

1. Fragmentary Order 1 to Operation Order 9–01, CNIK ETT, April 5, 2009, pages 2, 3, 4, and 5.

References

Campbell, Staff Sergeant Kyle. Counter Narcotics Infantry Embedded Team.

Cole, First Lieutenant Adam. Counter Narcotics Infantry Kandak Embedded Training Team.

Department of the Army, Assault Forwards 6, Headquarters and Headquarters Company, 3rd Battalion, 130th Infantry Division Regiment, Fort Riley, Kansas 66442.

Department of the Army, Counter Narcotics Infantry Kandak Embedded Training Team (CNIK EET), Camp Dubs, Darulaman, Afghanistan, APO AE 09320.

Kemper, First Lieutenant Troy. Counter Narcotics Infantry Kandak Embedded Training Team.

Mays, First Lieutenant Brian. Counter Narcotics Infantry Kandak Embedded Training Team.

Merseal, Major Kurt. Counter Narcotics Infantry Kandak Embedded Training Team.

Ressel, Staff Sergeant James. Counter Narcotics Infantry Embedded Team.

Settle, Captain Gregory. Counter Narcotics Infantry Kandak Embedded Training Team.

Sowash, Sergeant First Class Jeffery. Counter Narcotics Infantry Embedded Team.

Strong, Sergeant First Class Greg. Counter Narcotics Infantry Embedded Training Team.

Sury, First Sergeant John. Counter Narcotics Infantry Embedded Training Team.

Williams, First Lieutenant Jason. Counter Narcotics Infantry Kandak Embedded Training Team.

Index

Abdullah, Khadahari 3, 96
Abdullish, Mullah 3, 96, 153
Afghanistan, Helmand Province 3, 8, 13, 15, 17, 21, 126, 131, 132, 134, 152
Afghanistan, Kabul 5, 6, 124, 134, 147
Afghanistan, Kandahar 125
Afghanistan, Lashkar Gah 5, 17, 19, 148
Afghanistan, Marjah 132
Afghanistan, Nad Ali 19, 21, 32, 44, 46, 59, 61, 67, 70, 72, 74, 75, 76, 83, 94, 103, 121, 132
Afghanistan National Army's Narcotics Infantry Kandak (ANA CNIK) 3, 4, 5, 6, 8, 12, 14, 15, 21, 46, 56, 68, 70, 80, 83, 91, 93, 94, 96, 97, 98, 114, 119, 120, 123, 127
Afghanistan National Police's Poppy Eradiation Force 3, 5, 14, 29, 46, 56, 68, 70, 80, 91, 94, 96, 97, 98, 102, 113, 119, 120
AGS-17 Grenade Launcher 3, 8, 49, 52, 53, 131
Ahmed, Haroom 33, 83, 121
Allah, Farid 154
Anderson, Kegan 56, 83, 87, 96, 98, 103, 106, 122, 152

Bailey, Robert 67, 74, 152
Blough, Matthew 152
Brewer, Bill 14, 83, 96, 98, 110, 121, 122, 151

Camp Bastion 29, 113, 119

Camp Dubs 5, 125, 136
Camp Julian 125
Camp Phoenix 5, 11, 113
Camp Tombstone 119
Campbell, Kyle 23, 24, 28, 29, 50, 52, 67, 73, 77, 98, 117, 121, 122, 131, 142, 151
Cole, Adam 7, 8, 10, 12, 13, 17, 25, 33, 35, 37, 40, 43, 44, 64, 67, 70, 74, 80, 83, 87, 88, 96, 97, 98, 103, 108, 113, 116, 121, 122, 123, 135
Counter Narcotics Infantry Kandak Embedded Training Team (CNIK ETT) 3, 4, 5, 21, 69, 70, 73, 78, 80, 81, 83, 87, 91, 93, 94, 95, 96, 98, 102, 114, 119, 120, 121, 123, 127, 150
Coventry, Staff Sergeant 102, 113

Darokhan, Ramin Barack 33, 152
DynCorp International Poppy Eradication Force 3, 5, 6, 11, 13, 21, 30, 32, 33, 40, 44, 45, 46, 49, 50, 56, 59, 68, 69, 70, 73, 76, 78, 79, 80, 83, 85, 91, 92, 93, 96, 97, 98, 102, 106, 112, 114, 118, 119, 120, 137, 143

82MM Mortar 3, 4, 153, 154

Falmier, Freddy 12, 26, 33, 35, 68, 83, 88, 96, 98, 109, 121, 125, 151
FOB Dylan 5, 22
Fort Chaffey 129
Fort Riley, Kansas 129, 136, 142, 143, 144, 147

Index

Foth, Mark 33, 74, 88, 96, 98, 121, 151
Forward Observation Base (FOB) Eagle 3, 16, 20, 30, 41, 45, 53, 60, 69, 89, 93, 96, 97, 98, 123, 124, 154

Garcia, Michael 10, 23, 26, 27, 28, 29, 33, 49, 67, 74, 88, 93, 96, 117, 118, 152
Gershk City 97, 106, 110, 111, 117
Ghani, Colonel 97

Hadi, Abdul 154
Haroom, Ahmed 152

IED Factory 4, 97, 154
Illinois Army National Guard, 2nd Battalion, 130th Infantry Regiment, 33rd Infantry Brigade 3
Iraq 1 143

Johnson, Nick 49, 50, 88, 101, 137, 151

Kazada 154
Kemper, Troy 5, 27, 88, 92, 98, 111, 121, 126, 144, 151
Knootz, Thomas 152

Laos, Myanmar 2
Latin America 2

M-4 carbine rifle 4
Mark 19 grenade launcher 4, 24, 29, 33, 44, 49, 50, 51, 52, 69, 77, 96, 131, 149, 153
Mays, Brian 24, 32, 33, 38, 39, 48, 67, 83, 87, 93, 121, 126, 134, 139, 151
McLean, Anthony 152
McReynolds, Carter 152
Merseal, Kurt 5, 6, 7, 8, 10, 11, 12, 13, 14, 18, 19, 24, 25, 27, 29, 30, 34, 37, 38, 39, 42, 45, 49, 50, 51, 52, 53, 54, 55, 56, 69, 70, 73, 74, 79, 83, 84, 87, 89, 90, 96, 103, 106, 108, 111, 116, 117, 118, 121, 123, 128, 129, 137, 141, 151
Messick, Mason 152
Milliken, Ryan 152

Mirab 92, 121
Moden, Alam 154
Mohammad, Lai 4, 154
Mohammand, Ibrahimi 152
Mohammand, Omar Mullah
Mohammand, Suhrab 152
Moreno, Paul 121, 122
MRAP Cougar
Mujahideen 1

Nazer 154
Nirab 67
Noor, Mahammad 23, 33, 49, 93, 96, 121, 152
Noori, Mustafa 33, 49, 83, 98, 121, 152

Rabbitt, Sean 23, 34, 50, 51, 67, 99, 151
Ressel, James 12, 23, 33, 43, 49, 57, 67, 74, 88, 92, 93, 96, 98, 121, 122, 140, 151
Rowton, Nathaniel 152

St. Louis, Missouri 128
Sandell, William 12, 23, 25, 26, 28, 33, 46, 49, 56, 67, 69, 74, 92, 96, 98, 103, 105, 107, 122, 126, 151
Schuh, Michael 121, 122
Seair, Ahmad 152
Samir, Ahmad 96, 98, 152
Sessin, Kirk 83, 84
Settle, Greg 12, 14, 15, 21, 24, 25, 33, 38, 39, 40, 41, 46, 47, 48, 50, 53, 55, 56, 59, 61, 62, 63, 64, 65, 67, 69, 70, 73, 74, 77, 78, 83, 84, 87, 88, 89, 93, 101, 105, 107, 116, 121, 122, 134, 135, 139, 142, 151
Shah, Qahaj 154
Shakir, Abdul 152
Shurab 98
Southworth, Jared 44
Soviet Invasion of 1969–70 1
Soviet Union 1
Sowash, Jeffery 12, 23, 30, 33, 36, 45, 49, 57, 67, 117, 121, 123, 151
Springs, Quincy 56, 69, 101, 121, 151
Steelville, Missouri 128
Strong, Greg 7, 8, 12, 16, 18, 22, 31, 33,

Index

34, 42, 45, 46, 47, 48, 54, 56, 59, 61, 62, 64, 65, 67, 68, 70, 72, 73, 78, 83, 85, 86, 88, 91, 92, 93, 94, 98, 99, 102, 103, 114, 120, 121, 123, 126, 138, 151
Sury, John 12, 53, 54, 55, 79, 89, 90, 92, 96, 98, 107, 110, 114, 116, 117, 121, 151

Taliban 1, 2, 3, 7, 24, 25, 27, 33, 36, 37, 38, 39, 41, 43, 44, 45, 49, 50, 52, 55, 59, 68, 69, 73, 78, 93, 96, 111, 112, 130, 143
Thailand 2
3rd Brigade, 205th Corps 41
Third World Nationals (TCNs) 16
Thorpe, William 88, 93, 98, 152
Thoele, Scott 102, 113
Tyminski, Zachery 10, 26, 48, 121, 152

Ullah, Aman 4, 154
Ullaq, Shams 4, 154
United Nations Office on Drugs and Crime (UNODC) 2

Vietnam 150

Wahed, Lt. Col. 47, 49
Williams, Jason 10, 33, 61, 64, 80, 84, 96, 98, 101, 125, 151
Worker, Jason 96, 98, 105, 106, 110, 152

Zabullah, Sah 67, 74, 88, 99, 121, 152, 154
ZSU-23 anti-aircraft gun 3, 49, 123

www.ingramcontent.com/pod-product-compliance
Ingram Content Group UK Ltd.
Pitfield, Milton Keynes, MK11 3LW, UK
UKHW021846140426
5217IPUK00022B/1623